The Next God

by
Eva Ravenwood

EVA'S READING ROOM

Eva's Reading Room
Atlanta, Georgia

The Next God
by Eva Ravenwood
Published by Eva's Reading Room
P.O. Box 50473 - Atlanta, Georgia 30302
www.evaravenwood.com
e-mail – evaravenwood@yahoo.com

This book is intended to provide alternative spiritual thinking to those searching for answers they have not yet found. It will hopefully provide hope to those who feel that they are alone, floating with no destination.

Library of Congress Control Number: 2009900687

Ravenwood, Eva, 1953
The Next God

ISBN - 10: 0-9678469-2-7
ISBN - 13: 978-0-9678469-2-7
1.
Printed in the United States of America

May we all walk closer to God's brilliant light!

This book is dedicated to all those people who have hidden their communications with God, and other continued spirits, out of fear of being viewed as crazy. It is dedicated to the courage of those who boldly come out of the closet, and those who benefit from such communicators.

It is also for those people in "hazing", like my mother, who never quite figure out what is happening, and are too afraid to question the official mental health diagnosis that has been placed upon them. There are many.

also

for Troop
His patience and support have carried me far. I pray that he will sustain his present walk on the Light side

and
for Gwen
for whom I have eternal appreciation for her supportive heart, and endless expectation for her full growth

both are dearly loved!

FOREWORD

There are many books on the market spanning the intricate breadth of spirituality and how we as humans are woven into this complicated tapestry. Eva's revelations are as powerful as any and the clarity with which "deep" subjects are made plain, a gift.

For those who have consciously been on their path for decades to those of us who are taking their first conscious steps, **The Next God** is a must read ... perhaps more than once. It is books like this that help us define our true selves, our spiritual selves, and at the same time command we have humility in our hearts during this amazing journey.

As effectively, if not more powerfully, Eva like Neale Donald Walsch and his Conversations With God, assures us of Mother/Father/God's existence and that we are never alone. And if it is in God's plan for us, if is our time to truly talk to God by whatever means necessary, it shall be done.

Gwyn F. McGee aka Eboni Snoe
Author of "When Everything's Said and Done"
and "Something Deep in My Bones"

INTRODUCTION

This book is intended for the benefit of those readers within my Study Group. You will know if you are included in that group, because if not, this work will make no sense to you fairly quickly. If there are enough "hmmms", and "okay" during the reading of the first four chapters, we are probably related . . . from a Study Group standpoint. If this information is too simple for you, then you have probably moved beyond the point where I am and the information I am given. If this information is too odd or strange for you, then you may not have reached this point yet. I completely accept that the information I've been given is the interpretation that God wants me and those comfortable in my Study Group to have. However, God may provide other interpretations for other Study Groups. That is the way of our world.

The conclusions I have drawn and the messages I attempt to relate here are taken from many different sources from both spirits on our plane, and those who have continued or who are on another. I try not to interpret things that are best told directly. However, I do try and extrapolate information and design possible procedures from a culmination of many sources. I have tried to be clear about the difference between direct and indirect extrapolations, but of course what is clear in my head may lack clarity to the reader. I've realized this fact while working with my editors. I apologize for any confusion while I strive for clarity and understanding.

This book is a guide for those who can relate. As such, it can provide another perspective for those who are seeking new understanding. This can almost be assumed if you are voluntarily reading this or, as in the case of Troop (you'll understand later in the book), if you are being forced to read this. The statement "God moves in mysterious ways" is a gross understatement. If you are resistant to information that you don't already know or have some belief in, you are not likely to read very far. If you are diligent and read on, even in this state of mind, you are likely to try and rearrange the information to fit terms and concepts with that which you are already familiar. Unfortunately, without flexibility, no new information will be likely to penetrate. Thus, I hope you will remain as neutral as possible and get the most benefit from the words within.

I speak only from my point of view, unless I am speaking to you from what has been told to me. I am aware that everyone will not see or value things this way. However, if this information is useful to you, I am honored to be the messenger.

Please notice that I use the terms He, She and It interchangeably when referring to God, The Divine Architect or The Creator, if you prefer. I do that because that is the way I am presented with these references. I figure that we might as well all get the same treatment. In that vain, I have also noticed that I am not alone in hearing, or feeling and conveying the concepts within this book. Apparently, many people are now writing about these same messages from different perspectives. I believe we are headed toward a spiritual revolution and have been given information to share with the world. This new spiritual makeup of the world can change through the dissemination of this sometimes revolutionary information. Just as the people in "Close Encounters of the Third Kind" built the mountain/rock formation out of mud, mashed potatoes and their art and paintings, we, the messengers and telephone lines of psychic and spiritual communication, are being given similar messages and must make them available to all who will hear.

If you have questions or suggestions, please send them to me at evaravenwood@yahoo.com, as I will attempt to incorporate them in the writing of future books.

I thank you and may peace and brilliant light guide our journey together.

Eva Ravenwood

ACKNOWLEDGEMENTS

I would like to thank my editors, L. N. Coleman., for her hard work and endless support, and M. Barner Anselmi for her diligence and insight.

I am also grateful to the my test readers for their suggestions and feedback through all three incarnations and titles, and several years of developing this book, including some early readers, but not limited to Kevin Hicks, Carl Nunn, Patrice Coleman, Tua Nefer, Millicent Small, Tony Small, Danah Hilden, Hugh Marshall, Debra Francis, Jamilah Shakir, Jan Volz, Ruchelle White, Kai Bullard and the many clients who have read and critiqued the book for the two years it has been used as a guide for them to better understanding their readings.

I thank you, the reader, for your open mind. I suspect you and I will really need such in the coming thirty to forty years while we undergo spiritual reform. Ahead of time, I want to thank you for making the changes to envision a new world, as we develop it together with our spiritual connection, minds and hearts.

I greatly appreciate Dr. Emily Simerly, Dr. Mary Nell Chestnut, and Dr. Shawn Garrison for advice, guidance, clinical explanations and interpretations.

The wonderful work of Carl W. Nunn and W.A. Bridges for their wonderful photography, as well as Bill Alger and Hugh Marshall for the cover design, could not be more spectacular, and I am quite grateful.

I thank my many friends and family for being my anchors through very rough times while I was wrestling with control of this, and for always caring about my well being and showing it in a myriad of ways. You are all appreciated greatly.

Not enough words can be said about my gratitude to and for my son Alvis Baynes for his steady skepticism and watchful eye in the early years, and for having the good sense to know when it was time to relax in the self evident later years.

I appreciate beyond measure, all of the many clients, in the thousands now, who have helped me learn the parameters of this gift, and how to best deal with it. Without them, I nor the hypothesis in this book, could have developed very far, and I would not have come to some of these realizations. I thank you for your bravery, steadfastness even in the face of amazement and dismay, and the courage to tackle some very difficult life's challenges. Mostly, I thank you for not killing the messenger at times when it appeared that you at least wanted to curse her out. Your growth and dedication to that growth humbles and astounds me.

Enough cannot be said for the work of the Voice Hearer's Network in both the U.S.A. and England, and the Iccarus Project for their fearless, tireless work with people brave enough to speak out about their experiences. They are bold and courageous!

In keeping, I have learned tremendously from a local voice hearers group here in Atlanta that we started at the beginning of 2008. They are incredibly intelligent about their journeys and becoming very clear in their direction. Observation of how they work with their abilities and the benefits and sometimes difficulties that come with them has been crucial to my understanding of the melding between these worlds -- the spirit and emotional/mental parts of ourselves. I thank them for allowing me to be part of them. One very essential thing I have learned is that it takes a great deal of education for the non-hearers to fully understand these sometimes squirrelly abilities, and that while we are learning ourselves, we must be vigilant in working to help those who do not understand, to grasp a clearer picture of what is happening than the standard explanations. I thank this group for their fearlessness.

TABLE OF CONTENTS

CHAPTER ONE
I CAN'T BELIEVE I'M WRITING THIS

I have had at least five false starts with writing this book. I realize now that I have done everything I could think of to avoid writing it and feel most inadequate to do so. I don't want anyone to think that I consider myself an authority on this subject, despite my information source. Nor do I want people to take the information I impart and go off half cocked (as people are prone to do) with a lack of understanding and try and act upon any of this information without exercising proper reason. It is that concern, or should I say "fear", that has made me far more reluctant than I should have been to embark upon this endeavor. I would have been perfectly comfortable just wallowing in that state of inactivity for a few more years (despite the fact that I was **told** to write this book) had I been allowed to stay there.

Therein lies the problem: When God tells you to do something, He is patient beyond most human comprehension. However, when She is through, She is through, and things will not stay the same while we do our best to ignore and avoid the lessons put before us. The situation is likely to get very uncomfortable. Things start to fall apart and go haywire in one's life, and we usually don't understand why since we were perfectly happy staying right where we were, running in place. What's wrong with a treadmill anyway? It makes you feel like you are going somewhere, doesn't it?

Since I seem not to be able to avoid this task, this burden, this potential nightmare, I guess I have to just do what I am told; otherwise, my little world might get even more uncomfortable than it is already, God forbid-- literally.

Completing the task of writing this book has certainly not been easy because people are regularly locked up for what I'm about to say. Lock them up and throw away the key! At the least, people look at you like you are just left of sane and hold their children close when they see you coming. I'm partially kidding, because till the release of this book with my first ever photo as Eva, not thirty people in the world have known who I really am or that I might be just left of sane because I haven't come out of my spiritual closet much. Well that is changing now, and I am stepping out literally, on faith. This is a big step for me, so I'm glad you are taking it with me.

Like many in this position, I have been accused of being a Godsend when the information suits those I read for, to being demonic when it is in conflict with what they want to hear or do. And this, remember, is from the group that cares about me. Why in the world would I want to come out of this closet? Can you tell me? Believe me when I say this. It is only under great duress!

My saving grace has been the good that I have been able to do for my clients as my circle of service has expanded to include people all over the world now. So I am far more confident as time passes, with each new client and each of their successes.

Three people in my family went to mental institutions because they heard voices no one else heard. I have avoided being near any behavior that might result in similar incarceration, but it appears that this avoidance will not be allowed.

I talk to God and a lot of other folks too including: Angels, Guardian Angels and Spirits, Saints, Orisha, deceased relatives, some friendly and unfriendly ghosts, spirits and residual spirits (I keep that group to a minimum once I learned how), and the like, thus far. Animals are not exempt, but it works differently. The only difference from these communications and everyday, "normal" communications with most people is that the deceased, etc. all talk back and I can hear them. I don't hear in suggestions, or phrases, or a random word here and there, like "turn around", or "run", though that is how it happened most often when I was a young girl. I hear them loudly and as clearly as if you were reading the words on this page aloud. And, unlike some have described, it is not a quiet, "inner voice" that is indistinguishable from my own. The voices I hear are varied, male, female, young, old, deep and light, and can have accents. God's voice; however, is different.

I've tracked these conversations over the past few years and written down nearly every word. What I've found is that after the first year and a half or so of strong clairaudience, the things that have been said to me have proven to be about 85% accurate. If you allow for the bizarre time difference, and name differences that occur in strange places, about 90% are ultimately accurate.

Just to be clear, the time differences can look like this example: I may be told that a person I haven't seen or talked to in three years will come to visit one week after the 4th of July. That person does not come that year, but even though I still haven't talked to them, they do call in June two years later, and actually come to visit that year, on the 11th of July. This example actually happened. Apparently, time does not have the same meaning in the spirit world, and time continuum is not just theory.

Name and gender differences seem to run with reincarnations, and really are still a time issue dilemma. I will be told by my spiritual sources that a person's name and/or gender is one thing, and then when I talk with the actual person, this information is so wrong that it makes me question my sanity--which for a while was not a difficult task! I will then be told that the advising spirit is sorry, but that it was the person's name in a former or future incarnation. Apparently, I don't have enough problems working this out on my own, huh?

So, I guess I just threw the door open, sort of, and these are the confessions of a closet Direct.

CHAPTER TWO
WHAT IS A "DIRECT"?

A Direct is a clairaudient who hears God directly, first hand, in complete sentences. Before we go further, let me say that my definitions come from all these folks on the other side and God. I attempted to read a few books on the topic, but often they are written by well meaning clairvoyants or clairsentients and, given my personality, I need exact verbiage--even when I can't fully understand it. I figure that me interpreting them, and them interpreting what they felt was a bit much. Additionally, people--including myself--interpret through their own experiences. The trick is to learn to be strictly only a telephone receiver, and not an interpreter as much as possible. As a Direct, my biggest job has been to make sure that I do not add myself into the listening equation. That is no easy task either because God's voice does not sound like your Aunt Jane, or even like the Saints. The messages are not completely clear sometimes either, because that is part of the lesson, and the lessons never stop. Most messages are designed to make you think and grow, and may come in an almost riddle format.

I began to hear God clearly in 2001, which sent me running into the street until I literally understood Martha Reeves and the Vandella's song, "Nowhere to Run, Nowhere to Hide" (I didn't say I was any brighter than anyone else, only that I can hear!). In fact, I think that it is best to give you my interpretation of what is happening in some subjects, after years of listening, and then give you the present day words straight from the source in some cases. That way you will understand why I want to stay in the closet. Were this journey of hearing God as easy as most religions want to make it, the simplified version, then more folks would and could do it.

This is what I understand about being a Direct. Apparently there are 40,000 of us in the world. When I said that to a Muslim woman in my Study Group (we'll talk about that later), she said, "That's a significant number. I know I've read it in the Qur'an." I didn't look for this reference, so I don't know what she was trying to remember. Even though there are 40,000 of us who hear God clearly as if She were standing next to us, everyone has the ability to hear God. I don't know why the number whom can hear God directly seems to maintain at that specific number. I am unclear as to whether the rest of the 40,000 don't recognize their skill or don't choose to develop this ability, or do or not, though I do know that as part of a university project I am a participant of, one of the questions is about who we talk to, and the categories include God, ghosts, aliens, angels, spirit guides and a few other continued spirits. Otherwise, I haven't yet asked for this answer in full.

While everyone has the ability to communicate with God, it appears that everyone does not have the ability to communicate with much of the rest of the spirit world and can't necessarily hear Uncle James, and not as many can do both. So the question becomes: Why is this true, and why such a finite or perhaps definite number of Directs? I was told that if I took my chicken self on this journey of writing this book, I would begin to know what questions to ask in order to take me to the next level. I never asked that specific question before, so because God is all-wise, I can see as usual, that She is right, and that I will learn from this writing/questioning experience. I also see that taking this journey with you, the reader of this book, might just turn into a pleasant experience.

At any rate, clairaudients – people who hear; clairvoyants – people who see; and clairsentients – people who feel strongly, and there are some other categories as well, can receive these messages in various ways and varying degrees of accuracy. I am all three, but the clairvoyance disturbs me, so I asked to be relieved of that for a while until I can handle it better. I spent most of my childhood and early adulthood seeing folks others could not. I can't tell you how many times I ended up asking people some version of "Do you see the man sitting in the corner with the blue shirt on, smoking the pipe?" And when they would say, "No, what man?" or whatever the situation, though he might still be there, looking right at me, my answer would be, "Hummmm, me neither now. He must have gone outside." Gratefully, I got better at being slick with the questions. Sometimes I just didn't ask anymore and would move closer to the entity which usually made them disappear.

When the movie, "The Sixth Sense" by M. Night Shyamalan came out, I was dating a man from Africa who had been raised to be a spiritual leader but had rejected his training in his late twenties. However, he was very knowledgeable about spiritual matters and recognized me for what I was even before I fully grasped it. He would dream at night while sleeping next to me, and in the morning I could tell him parts of his dreams. Other times I would dream about his family members and see them clearly. I did learn to temper my visions on one occasion because I frightened him with one of my interpretations and made him unduly concerned about his father. I learned to keep some things to myself from that incident until I could figure out what they meant. Interpreting dreams is a multilevel journey in which one becomes more exact and clear all the time—only to have the lessons get more complex.

Again, dreams and feelings were too inaccurate for me. I think it was that aversion to inaccuracy that helped me achieve greater clairaudient skills. God lets you learn at your own pace to some degree, as long as you keep moving forward. It worked the same way in clairvoyance for me. I have never liked horror movies, so seeing parts of people or finding my dead friend standing in my doorway really did not work for me. At one time, a deceased friend climbed into bed with me for two weeks straight until I figured out to get rid of the pack of cigarettes he left in my house the day before he was killed in a car accident (more on that incident later). Had that continued, I believe I would have snapped and ended up in a mental institution like my mother or my aunts. So I asked for this clairvoyance ability to be put on hold, and it was granted, happily. However, avoiding communication didn't work with writing this book.

I believe I became a Direct for two reasons. The first is because my life has always been absurdly difficult, and I needed help navigating. Secondly, I was in turmoil from all of this difficulty coming to a head. In order to cope, I went out in the woods and sat by a beautiful creek and prayed from two to eight hours a day, at least four times a week, for two years. I had too many mixed messages, too many coincidences, too many voices in my head that were unclear, and too many bizarre things happen to ignore. Afraid that I might end up schizophrenic like my mother, I did the only thing I could think of: I pleaded for help from God, from my ancestors, from the Saints and the Orisha (who are actually the same, depending on your culture or religion).

One day my fraternal grandmother appeared, sitting on a rock that was jutting up from the creek and watched me. I had never met her and had only seen pictures as she died before I was born. She was quiet, and she watched me patiently. She spoke to me without moving her lips, as others had done before. But the difference was that I could hear every single word, and not just from thought phrases as I had done previously. Before that time, I only sensed, though completely, what was meant by the spirit/person. I was fascinated and frightened at the same time. She was clear as a bell and looked as solid as my own flesh.

She told me not to be afraid, that I was about to learn and understand so many new things. My fear subsided as she informed me that if I stayed open-minded and clear, all manner of information would be coming my way, and I would gain the clarity I had been praying for. She was my first completely clear communication and the precursor for becoming able to hear God directly. From that point on over the next year, things really heated up and I moved from this first undeniable communication to my moment on the porch when God spoke to me without doubt!

I'm skipping a lot here, because much went on before that day, however I want to make the concept of becoming a Direct clear.

I believe God allowed me to become clairaudient because of these factors:

1. I worked very hard to gain clarity so I could move past the point my mother and aunts had gone, as I was certain that if I didn't, I'd end up in a mental institution.
2. I was born in a bloodline that was allowed this ability with possibly more ease than some other people – in essence bred for this.
3. I never believed that the Christian teachings I grew up with were enough to explain the true nature of God, and always, for as long as I can remember, needed to move past elementary explanations that seemed designed to control people rather than inform them and make their relationship with God their full responsibility. This led me to believe from the age of twelve that religion and most adults were not equipped to

explain to me what and who God was, because they themselves lived and operated with inadequate assumptions which they allowed to guide their daily lives. I wasn't sure what God was, but I was sure that the explanations I was hearing weren't fully formulated.

4. God is pure, brilliant energy and communication with Him is all about the capability and methodology of the energy exchange. If you do the things that alter your energetic vibrations, and prayer is one method to do that, you can change your frequency and vibrate at a different rate that allows you to pick up things that others cannot. As a child, I could hear alarm systems that only dogs could hear, so apparently, by staying in prayer so long, I enhanced my ability to hear other frequencies even more.

5. I have always had the ability to clear the noise out of my head naturally. This, I gather from the little bit of studying meditation methods that I have done, is what people are learning to achieve when they meditate. At an early age, I could go dumb (not a thought in my head) at a moment's notice, and maintain this status for a very long time, clearing out all thoughts, noise, sounds, head noise and anything else in the way. That is the state that you must achieve in order to hear continued spirits and/or God. I call it the "automatic tennis ball theory", which I will explain later.

Thus, after all this considerable transformation I was able to achieve through concerted effort, I was led to the incident that occurred on my front porch. On this particular day I began to hear an overwhelming multi-voice with dozens of tones and pitches all speaking to me at once. I asked who it was, and it said in a multitude of female, male and children's voices at once, "I am what you would call God."

CHAPTER THREE
TURNING ON THE SWITCH

To hear God speak directly is a unique dichotomy: on one hand it is not hard at all, and on the other hand it is very difficult. Successful communication requires a specific state of mind and spirit. In order to hear God, you must condition yourself emotionally and spiritually to accept how absolutely miniscule you truly are. You must also realize the insignificance of your thoughts, actions, state of being and plans. When you have achieved this alteration in state of mind and spirit and relinquished control over your own plans, then communication with God seems to have a better chance. As long as you think you are running and designing events in your life, you might have difficulty because your own ego is taking up too much space. Of course, I did not transition straight from "I see dead people" as a child, to hearing God. There was a very definite progression for me in my path to understanding.

I always knew there was something not quite right in my family. These mental/emotional problems were evident in both my mother and fathers' families. My father was too overbearing, too controlling, and though he was very kind, there was something way off about the manner in which he felt he needed to rule us. Unfortunately, he thought it was appropriate to destroy our self esteem on some levels. Additionally, we were a family of five girls, and that seemed to make him furious. Not a boy in sight, and he resented it.

One of my sisters was very strange and is unlike anyone I've ever met. As a teenager she constantly wore black clothes, pasty make up, was quite spacey, and she was never on the same wave length as the rest of the world. She was alternately docile and then mean as a snake, but mostly, she danced to a very, very different tune. People referred to her as "very odd."

My parents divorced when I was 12. Just prior to the divorce, my father took my younger sister and me to the Midwest where we lived with my aunt for almost one year. I suspect he did this out of spite and after fighting with my mother for months about custody of us children. It was a devastating experience for all of us. Losing this battle with my father was particularly harmful for my mother, and she began to experience some emotional problems. My sister, the strange one, 18 at the time, was the only person at home with mother, as the two older daughters had already left home. That's one version of the story, and the only one I knew for many years, but not all there was.

This sister called my father one night and said quite calmly, "Mother is having some serious problems, and I think you should come home." Inexplicably, my father packed us up and we moved back home. The sight of him made my mother hostile, angry and too volatile, so he allowed us to stay with her while he stayed with my aunt a couple of miles away. Things seemed calm at first, then Martin Luther King, Jr. was assassinated. My mother cried as if she had lost a parent for about a week and a half. It was not a good sign. My odd sister seemed incredibly calm, enough for my father to comment about how composed she was. I found her demeanor peculiar.

As the days went by, my mother escalated into a frenzied state. She became quite paranoid and thought we were listening to her phone conversations. She cried, couldn't go to school, read the Bible constantly and finally one night she told us to go get the ladder so she could climb up on the roof to tell everyone that Jesus was coming back. At the time she was probably 230 pounds, and not in the best physical shape Well we danced all around that request for obvious reasons. Then she proceeded to hit the walls with her hands, causing massive cracks in the plaster as she "preached" from the Bible for the next five or six hours while screaming "Satan, get thee back" at the top of her lungs. Now it might be more clear why I wasn't so quick to fling this door of spiritual awareness and intervention open, right?

We called my father who called our doctor. People who are schizophrenics or who are in altered energy states can have incredible physical strength. After much effort, a couple of hurt orderlies, a broken window and quite a bit of drama, they subdued her, put her in a straight jacket and then in an ambulance and took her away to a mental institution. My two sisters who were home at that point were devastated and crying. Strangely enough, like my odd sister, I felt quite calm and can't remember crying at all.

My mother was institutionalized for several months. After she was allowed to return home my parents did not reconcile because she did not want to. My odd sister had gotten married and left home and my mother, younger sister and I lived in our family home. Mother began working for the first time in her life, and as long as she took the medication for schizophrenia, she did fine, as far as we could tell. However, she had no life. She was in bed every night at 7 p.m., and the Thorazine she was prescribed was taking a toll on her heart. But she was calm. I, on the other hand, did not believe that schizophrenia as an explanation, was all that had happened.

From research and discussion with the continued spirits I have learned that many people who are not fully competent in "hearing" the continued spirits as kids, come into this awareness in mid-life, often during their 40s or 50s. My mother was 50 at this time. I know now that my mother heard things that she could not reconcile in her head, and thus checked out, emotionally speaking. After years of watching people diagnosed as schizophrenic, I believe now this probably happens much more frequently than we think. These unfortunate people cannot comprehend what is happening to them, so they leave in essence-- and turn it over to someone else to figure out.

My mother went to work and did fine until she decided she was doing so well that she no longer needed the medication. This seems to be common with some schizophrenics; however, I wish I had known enough to pay attention to whether or not there were patterns with the patients around her who also did this. What makes one schizophrenic decide to stop taking medication, and others never take that chance? My mother was a gambler in this way, so over the next few years, she tested this more than was comfortable. My other sisters were too busy or too uncomfortable being near the disorder and one was even afraid she might "catch" schizophrenia somehow. Thus, I was left to deal with mother most often as my father couldn't go near her during these times because she would become violent.

After her first institutionalization she asked me to promise that I would not let her go back to the mental institution. She wanted me to assure her we would try and keep her in the regular hospital until she could get straight. This amazing presence of mind was evidence to me that in her case, schizophrenia was not quite what the doctors described. It was shortly after this time that we had to hospitalize mother again.

I was almost fourteen, so I went to the mental ward of the regular hospital on the second day when they allowed me to see her. I walked in just as she was literally sliding a nurse down the hallway. The woman slid about 10 or 12 feet before she could stop herself. My mother who was 5 feet 9 inches and about 220 to 230 pounds at the time, had not knocked her down or hit her, but actually grabbed her by the back of her collar and the seat of her pants, lowered her and slid her as if she was a sack of potatoes. She only got floor burns and was not seriously hurt. They had not been prepared for my mother's strength. She seemed calm until they touched her that morning.

Shortly after the sliding of the nurse, several big orderlies came in and wrestled mother to the bed, strapped her in and gave her very large doses of tranquilizers, which made her somewhat subdued, but did not make her sleep. I stayed in the corner and watched. The hospital staff allowed this because when I was around my mother was calmer. I also seemed to be able to handle this situation. Normally children were not allowed in their parent's room during such situations. This proved to be my first clue of the unique connection I had with my mother.

As one of the nurses left the room, she turned and said "Honey your mother won't sleep. I don't care how much we give her, and we have given her enough to tranquilize a horse, she just won't sleep. If she doesn't sleep soon, we are going to have to transfer her to the state mental hospital or other facility. We are only for short-term care here, emergencies. I'm afraid she could stay like this for weeks." She patted me on my shoulder and left.

I certainly had my work cut out for me. My mother had made it clear that she did not want to end up in a mental institution, so I had to think of what to do in order to honor this request. I sat in a chair next to her, closed my eyes, held her hand, and willed her to sleep. First I said it out loud, asking her to just try and sleep. I soon realized that the sound of my voice made her more alert, and she was working herself into a more aware state. So I thought the sentence, and repeated it in my head like a mantra. "Just sleep Ma, or they will take you away. Please go to sleep." I tried to think of it as a cord from me to her, from my voice to her head as if constantly pumping the word "sleep" straight into her forehead, about where I now know the third eye is located. This was one of those amazing messages God sends us of which we are unaware.

As long as I could concentrate on her sleeping, she did. If I was distracted by someone walking in the room, or by a thought about school or something frivolous like a party that weekend, she would wake up. It took me about four hours to realize this effect, so I learned to clear my mind (the tennis ball theory you'll hear of later) of all other thoughts, and only think of her sleeping. I even got to the point over the next two days where I could concentrate on speaking to my mother subconsciously, while carrying on a conversation with the nurse. It took effort, but I learned a lot about how our minds communicate on different levels, states and energy bands with that second exacerbation. As long as I focused, she slept, if I broke it she awakened. The staff tried to run me out of the room several times, telling me I was too young to spend that much time in a hospital room. They finally figured out that she was calm and sleeping over the next three days while I was there, so they left me alone when I protested. I stayed over the weekend for 12 or 13 hours each day willing her to sleep. It worked and she was able to process the medication after about four days. She was able to leave the hospital and return home within two weeks.

During this time, I learned some very important lessons:

- People don't just communicate by mouth and voice
- We can control telepathic communication if we free our minds and think and operate differently
- My mother was probably not actually schizophrenic, but I didn't know what was happening to her
- My mother and I were connected unlike anything I had known of before, and shared a psychic link

I believe this was the true beginning of my awareness that there is an alternate reality connected with our own, and that regular, normal people could connect with it. Before that time, I had received some indications of my special abilities, like seeing people that others didn't see, almost howling at the moon from the high frequency of the alarm in some department stores, a voice or two saying something I couldn't quite make out, and a premonition or two that could be explained away as déjà vu or luck.

It would be years before I understood more, but my mother provided me more practice. She began to speak in code when she had her episodes, a code I was learning to interpret. By the time I was 20, I learned that she was emotionally checking out of life when things became more than she could handle. During these episodes, she would begin to rant in an incomprehensible pattern, putting things together that didn't belong. I finally discerned she was actually talking in her own code. For instance, if she talked about white chickens, she was afraid. If she talked about gorillas, she was being bullied or the problem was bigger than she could handle. Somewhere in between, she would actually say a word or two that was related to the actual problem that the spiritual/mental trip was designed to take her away from.

I learned to let her rant during the first day of her exacerbation, and sit with a pad and pen writing down the occasional word that seemed related. A typical rant might go something like "The gorillas in the trees were at the door and then the flies on the wall might too but Ms. Johnson said the trees were the place for the flowers." The trick word in there was Ms. Johnson. The issue was with her. I would then wait for the next sentence, and it might include animals, plants, shopping, and then somewhere in it I'd hear "bad review" and so on. By the end of the first day, I could usually figure out what threw her off kilter, and what she thought was too much for her to handle. Thus, the problem might be something like her getting a bad review at work from her new boss, and feeling bullied because the woman was known for coming in and cleaning house, though it was not the policy of the company. She was afraid of losing her job and couldn't figure out how to work around it. Once I was clear about it, I could tell her the two or three probable versions I'd come up with and let her know there were alternative ways to deal with her problems. I would help her figure out acceptable solutions and then will her to sleep, and she would sleep.

If I didn't get it right, she would rant some more until I did. She was unable to rest until the problem was uncovered, and I had responded with the right answer to the riddle, in her estimation. When I look back on this time period, it was truly a fascinating process. We developed our processes almost to a science, albeit an unusual parent/child situation. I'd figure out the issue, then will her to sleep for a couple of days, the medication would take effect, she would become lucid and she'd be out of the hospital within two weeks and wouldn't have to go to a mental institution. This was obviously not textbook schizophrenia. Additionally, when new doctors dealt with her, they talked about changing her diagnosis to manic-depressive (called bi-polar now) because she didn't quite fit the description. I'm convinced now that she was neither schizophrenic or manic-depressive.

This became our pattern for the next 15 or so years until she was not able to come back as easily because of her age. I was also more easily distracted and had less time to go home from my own city and family and assist during that crucial first week of her episodes. After her last full blown exacerbation at age 64, she had a hard time coming out of it. We had a long, serious conversation during which I said once again, as I had over the years, that she needed a better system to deal with the problems in her life. I was afraid she might not be able to come out of it again, and I might not be able to help her. We had never really talked too much about our system, other than her saying that I seemed to calm her and it seemed unusual. I never tried to have a full blown discussion with her because I felt certain it would frighten her, and I was fairly unsure what was happening beyond the obvious. I was very uncertain on how to broach this delicate subject with a fairly unstable woman. However the talk seemed to be enough, and she never chanced omitting her medication again.

Also at about age 20, I had my first full blown, long lasting, undeniable, non-fleeting encounter with a spirit that I could not possibly explain away. I was out on my own, divorced, raising a kid, in college and working. A friend I grew up with had just returned from Viet Nam. We'll call him Jeff. We were developing a new deepening twist to our relationship. No sparks yet, just warm feelings. He came over to my house on a Thursday night to tell me about a party on Friday night. While he was there, he opened a pack of cigarettes which he forgot and left on my coffee table. I put them in the kitchen cabinet to hold for him.

A girlfriend and I went to the party the next night, and he showed up with another woman who lived in his apartment complex. Jeff was very, very high, and I was beginning to realize that he, as many others, had come back from the war with a serious drug habit. Around midnight, we were leaving and we asked if he wanted us to take him home. He said no, he was fine. We insisted that he not drive. We suggested he allow the woman with him to drive home or else he needed to leave with us. We even offered to stay at the party until he was ready to go. He promised he would let the woman drive, and she promised to do so. We left.

The next morning at 6:30 am, someone called to ask if I had read about Jeff, and how he was killed the night before after leaving the party. He had allowed the other woman to drive home, but after she dropped him off in front of his apartment, he got in the car and took off alone. He subsequently hit a bridge support at an extremely excessive speed of 115 mph.

I was in a daze and overwrought. I couldn't believe it and called my girlfriend who'd attended the party with me and told her. We were both in shock, but for some morbid reason, I wanted to see his car. She found out where it was and took me to see it. It looked like a crumpled piece of paper. One of his shoes was lying in the front floorboard. I picked it up and stared at it. Bad move for a clairsentient with some intuitive abilities.

That night, I was lying in the bed, not really sleeping and thinking about what a waste it was for him to make it through Viet Nam, come home and then die so young, and how beautiful and talented he had been. He had been a gifted artist. Not suddenly, but most certainly, he appeared in the doorway, in full – not transparent, floating or wispy. I sat straight up in the bed, and though I was anxious, I didn't really feel all-out fear. He was clothed, yet (that is difficult to explain), his clothes seemed in shadow and difficult to see. Though I knew it was he, his face seemed to be in shadow also. He spoke without moving his lips though I could sort of feel/hear him, though not word for word like my grandmother. He said that I should not be afraid, and I should not feel so much sorrow. He was fine, and he would be fine. He stayed there for a few minutes until I was completely calm and then he just disappeared.

I felt unusually peaceful. I got up from the bed and walked into the hallway, past where he had stood, and through the entire house. He was gone. I went back to bed and slept well. I went through the next day uneventfully, and paid my respects to his family, talked with friends about him and went about the business of living. However, that night, he came back.

I was lying in bed, trying to drift off to sleep facing the side of the room where the door was located. I turned over, and he was lying next to me. I didn't reach out to touch him, but wanted to and was afraid to at the same time. He was as clear as a bell, looking at me, sort of smiling. He must have sensed my desire to touch him, and said to me, with no words spoken and no lips moving, I sensed him saying, "Don't try touching me, it will only frighten you when you can't." So I didn't.

We lay there for a while and he conveyed the message again that he was alright, and that he cared about me and was sorry that we didn't get to find out where we might have gone in a new kind of relationship. He again said he was alright, and then he was gone.

I didn't see him the next night. His funeral was the day after, nearly the last funeral (except for my Grandmother's) that I would attend for almost twenty-five years because of the impact it had. I had only been to one other funeral—my Godfather's-- when I was about eight. I could have sworn I saw two people and heard people talking whom I could not see during my Godfather's service, but nothing would prepare me for Jeff's funeral.

I went with two girlfriends, one of whom had been with me the night he died. The other was the friend who called the next morning and was directly behind me when we walked by the open casket. As we approached, I was getting the growing feeling that there were people in the room other than the ones I could see, but still I forged on. As we reached the foot of the coffin, I had a shaky feeling. As I reached the open part of the casket and saw his face, I couldn't believe what I saw. When he visited me at night, he was perfect, and looked wonderful as he had always been a beautiful man. Looking down on him against the satin folds of the inside of the casket, he was ashen, almost gray and his brown skin looked like a dusty elephant. There was a scar from his hairline that crossed his face from the upper right side down to his neck. It was deep, had been sewn up grotesquely. I was wondering what fool from his family had decided that casket should be open. Just as I was completing that thought, a cool gust of wind came up from his body and went through and past me with enough force to knock the wind out of me. My knees began to buckle. I started sinking to the floor when my girlfriend caught me from behind as I was going down. My friend in front of me turned and helped, and they must have gotten me to a chair. I just remember I was sitting when I regained composure.

Years later, I've come up with a couple of theories about what happened. Death doesn't frighten or alarm me, and never really did. I am now confident in my sense of what's after what we consider death, and for the most part and in most cases, it is actually more pleasant. However pain is a whole different issue. I have always been an empath, which means that if I am exposed to other people's or other spirits' pain I feel it deeply. I believe when I looked down at Jeff's face, I got a glimpse of the amount of pain he had to be in to sustain that type of injury. When I approached the coffin, I picked up on the pain vibrations that his body must have endured physically.

My second theory surrounding this experience is that because I was connected to Jeff and because I was possibly the only human spirit in the vicinity who could receive his vibrations, that I actually received his left over physical vibrations—sort of like a hologram if you will. These vibrations were able to either attach to me or be drawn to me. In other words, because I vibrated at a level that was different from most, Jeff's spiritual memory – not actual spirit, but more like an imprint of his spirit – was able to move in my direction with more force than I was prepared for, causing me to lose my vibratory and physical balance.

This interpretation and understanding all came about much later. All I knew at the time is when I saw him, something very real went through me, my knees went weak, people had to catch me, and I passed out for a couple of seconds!

I've learned in the past few years most spirits do not really linger here. Since my "full exposure" (what I call my full understanding and acceptance of my abilities) I've learned spirits pass on to wherever they are supposed to go. However, they can leave a hologram of themselves here for some specific time or until something happens to change their vibratory levels in their resting place, especially if they have unusually high, low or odd vibratory levels. The most important part of this is that we can affect spirit's vibrations, as we affect each other's all the time. We can send up beacons to connect to each other and other spirits, and we can attract them with vibrations we transmit. We can also hold a signal of sorts, through objects, that keeps their hologram, or residue spiritual signature, connected to us.

That night after the funeral, Jeff came back to visit me, but he didn't say much other than he was fine, and I should not be afraid. After being knocked to my knees at the funeral, I was afraid as I listened to him say basically the same things he'd told me during his previous visits. Still I had no reason to fear him exactly, only that it seemed he would be with me for the rest of my life, saying nothing particularly different, just trying to reassure me.

I began to understand that this apparition was not actually him, but some residue of him. It took me almost two weeks to calm down and figure out that something was holding his hologram or spiritual shadow to me that neither he nor I could control. I'd wake up and he'd be sitting on the edge of the bed, or lying next to me. It got to be so common that I got over the fear and tried to figure out what might be happening. Surely an active spirit should not be operating like a broken record, doing the same things over and over again, with no new information. He had no new agenda other than to comfort me, but in actuality, after that first couple of days, I was no longer afraid or uncomfortable, so what was the real point of these repeated visits?

That was when I realized that Jeff's cigarettes were still in the cabinet and must have been calling him somehow. Operating from the possibility that somehow I was keeping his spirit from passing on and finding peace, I wrapped the cigarettes up in a bag, said a small prayer that Jeff find peace and rest, and threw them in the trash can out on the street. And just like that, Jeff, or his hologram, was gone.

I figured out I was holding his vibration in my space, so that his residual vibrations were still attached to my house. He was not actually there, but his hologram was. And this hologram version of Jeff was sort of stuck on comforting me, as that was his general stance and concern for me. I waited with great trepidation for him to come back for a couple of months. He never reappeared, and I was able to relax.

What I learned at that time was not to keep stuff around that people who have passed on were attached to or left because they might hang around because of it. In my case, as all of our interactions had been pleasant, there were only pleasant interactions with Jeff's hologram. He also must have been at peace when he died, which I sensed at the time. I kept having this recurring feeling that he just wanted to see what would happen when he hit a bridge support at 115 miles per hour. I was sure he had been really high and feeling no pain at the time he tried it, and died so quickly after impact that he never became tormented or in pain. It was quick, swift and then gone, sort of like the residual fleeting sensation I picked up at his funeral. Extremely fast moving discomfort and then gone. Medical officials said Jeff died instantly—which is exactly what I sensed.

People who have lower vibrations and cannot actually see the departed but continue to hold on to the loved one's effects out of a desire to remain close to those who have passed may have a hard time moving on when the spiritual hologram is hanging around. I'm sure these individuals don't fully understand why they can't let go either, but I suspect they are holding the spirit residue to them in this form in order to keep the loved one who has passed closer. The departed loved one isn't really close, but the residual/hologram is. It is sort of like having a spiritual picture that really can't interact completely with you, but can be reassuring by their presence. That actual spirit is living its "continued" or "passed over" life, and may be trying to find someone like me to tell you to get on with yours. They may even have returned to earth in real spirit form and are reborn in reincarnated form.

I would like to clarify this difficult issue. I have experienced occasions in which an actual ghost/spirit—not the holographic spiritual image can be here on this plane. However, I think that scenario is much rarer and requires an incredible amount of energy work to accomplish either on the part of the earth-bound individual, or on the part of spirits on this side. This would not be a random spiritual situation, but a far more complex one. I'm not comfortable discussing this much more either, as I have no desire to call this test upon myself and have not asked for enough information about it to speak clearly about calling ghostlike forms, though some have visited of their own accord. From my experiences, ghosts still have a human/spirit form that seems displaced. Spirit visitations are energy that seems quite appropriately here, and not displaced. It may be a matter of intention. For the most part, I believe almost all the ghosts on the highways, or in houses who do the same thing over and over again are holograms of spirits, constituting ghostlike images. I have not asked many questions about this area, so this exploration will be educational for all of us.

However, there are at least two other categories of spirits with whom I have been in contact. They are, 1) unresolved spirits who are half here waiting for something to happen, not just reassuring, and, 2) active spirits who have something they want to accomplish, positive or negative, and they are not able to do so from the other side and so stay active here.

At any rate, these two incidents and situations alerted my journey as one that might be a bit different and marked the beginning of my switches being more acutely turned on, and the beginning of the road I am traveling.

I said I would ask spirits on the other side questions regarding my take on some situations. In this case, I decided that the best person to ask would be Jeff. Here are his responses:

Eva: Jeff, is my assessment of this information correct?

Jeff: Not entirely. I was thinking of you when I hit the bridge support, which is the reason that I think I stayed connected to you. It is an energy field that reaches from one being to another, and I was reaching out to you. My thought was at first to wonder how it might feel to hit the bridge support while being so high, but then at the last moment, I tried to pull the car back on course. I became slightly afraid, and then I became calm again. My last thought was that you and I would not be able to go any further with our relationship and that was not what I wanted. I wondered where it might go. I was thinking that when I hit. I believe now that the energy I exerted in that thought attached to you somehow, and because you already had the ability to connect with other kinds of energies, even though you didn't fully realize it, I was able to stay with you in part.

Eva: Were you really here or was it residual?

Jeff: It was more like a thought that could materialize whenever you also shared that thought. I could stay as long as you continued to wonder too what might have been. When you finally found it more important to have peace of mind than to wonder about your loss, I was no longer able to connect to you in that way. Now bear in mind that my full spirit was already resting for the journey and the new life on this side, but I was able to still have some part of me there.

Eva: So it is not a hologram.

Jeff: Not quite. It is more a mist of a part of the spirit, but it does not hurt the spirit not to have that small portion as we do not operate as solid beings as you think of yourselves. We operate more in particles that are transparent and translucent, that then fully realize the images that you might see. That is why we can have a few particles of ourselves in many places at once, and still gather them to us when we want to or need to and we can on the other hand leave them in places to give comfort if needed. That was what was happening to you in that case. You wanted to know that which was ended, and could no longer be known, as I had wanted to know in the split second before I hit the support. In your case, it held my particles of recognition, maybe that is the best way to describe it, till you sent them home. It was the physical act of sending me home that released the particles of thought, of essence, of connection more than getting rid of the cigarettes. It was that you released the need to know that which you could not know in that manner any more, and thus that allowed me to release my own, or rather maybe a good way to describe it was to collect my own matter back to myself and become whole again because you no longer needed that connection to me.

Eva: This cannot be the way that all ghosts work though, is it?

Jeff: No it is not the kind of thing you see in hauntings, or in spirits that need something. There are many different types and styles of connectivity that can occur between two spirits in the blink of an instant. There are some bound by love, as you and I were to some degree – the love we felt though budding, and the potential of love and loss of potential – those are the things that held us. But loss can also hold people and spirits together. I would venture to say that when you find a spirit/particle that is remaining like I did, in a negative situation there is a residual of loss or pain in the people that see them, if they are not directly connected to the spirit that left your plane. There is a pain connection as opposed to a love connection, and that person somehow identifies with the pain that the person who sees them has as well. That is why not all people see the ghost, but some people see them as clear as a bell. Again, that is not a full being left on your plane, but the spirit particles left there that were not able to get home for some reason back to the spirit on the other side. Many reasons are responsible for that, but still the fact remains that the person on your side who is connected to them shares some particle relationship. That is their draw to one another.

Eva: Let me be clear. If the spirits are losing particles, for lack of a better word, are they not losing themselves, and becoming un-whole?

Jeff: Not at all. The miniscule portion that it takes to render something like an image, even an active image could be unclaimed for many lifetimes and it still won't make a difference to the spirit. However at some point, that spirit will have to go reclaim the particles to be completely whole as it evolves, as once we move into the higher vibratory realms, we are in need of all particles so that we can do the work that we need. Think of it as you pressing your hand upon a piece of paper, and it leaving a fingerprint. If you were not doing anything too complex, that residue, the fingerprint, would mean nothing. But if you were doing something that you needed all the cells and all the possible energy and particles of your being to create something complex, you might not want to release those kinds of parts of your body and let them just hang around out there. You would collect all of those impressions and hold on to them for the more difficult work ahead. That is not the best example, but one that might make it make sense.

Eva: So the cigarettes meant nothing.

Jeff: Not true, but not exactly in the manner in which you described it. It was more the act of sending me on my way, and deciding not to think about me in terms of what might have been that made the bigger impact. That was because of the level at which you are working. However, if you were about to create a new planet, then we have a different scenario, and I'm not certain I understand all of what that might mean. It is very complex and all based on energy and even stray energy must be contained and accounted for, for the mission – the task. You will understand more in time. It is advanced even for this side to understand.

My comprehension of it is not full and realized. Be patient. There is much time to learn.

Eva: So I'm a little confused about the two ghost experiences I have had. The Ghost on the water and P.D.(who is discussed later, though the ghost on the water is not at this time). Can you explain them to me?

Jeff: The ghost on the water was the same sort of situation. He was attached to some particles there because there were some unresolved issues, and he was also still attached to a wife who would not let him go. You picked up his vibrations because he had two areas of unresolved issues - the murder on the water, and the wife on the other side of town. Both held him in different ways, so you were reading his particles that were residual, sort of like you are thinking, but they had no resolution. If you will remember, he tried to get you to help him resolve it so his particles could be released. That situation, because it was unjust, held him. You were able to release me and let me go, in other words move me out of your life. I didn't have many unresolved issues, so once you did so, and my mother did so, I had no stray particles hanging around on that plane. That was not true with him. He had many.

The other ghost/spirit you encountered was not a ghost at all, but a spirit from this side who willed her particles to stay in that plane so she could negatively affect energy on your side. You were able to release the participatory particles she had entwined on that side by your energy altering states, in other words, prayer raised the vibration enough for her to will herself free. She made the difference from this side, because you initiated the difference from that side and in effect released the bond to that side for her. Then she was free to choose to let go. She had locked herself into her repetitive and destructive behavior beforehand. It was her choice though to leave particles, more than others to have her there.

Eva: Thank you for this explanation. As I said, even with all the information, this is a journey designed for teaching. I'm not sure I understand all of this yet. Will you be back on this side soon?

Jeff: Probably not before the end of your lifetime, but not too long. I have many things left undone in my growth. Be well.

CHAPTER FOUR

EXISTING IN SEMI TURNED-ON MODE

Despite the fact that these have not been the every day experiences of most people, when you are living them, when many credible doctors, your father, most of your immediate community and mean schoolyard kids have told you that your mother is completely insane, you don't go around discussing these kinds of experiences openly. Additionally, the one person who would probably understand the experiences but can't control them and is therefore unstable, my mother, was far too fragile to discuss these situations. My odd sister, who I suspect was experiencing something even stranger, was too peculiar and far away to talk to. In this case, I suppressed all evidence of these oddities.

If I saw suspect people, I didn't even ask anymore as I had as a child. I just assumed that nobody else could see them if they were not acknowledged. Yet, it is difficult and unhealthy to deny or try and escape one's true self. I began to develop other abilities. I worked alongside many women for years and invariably, long before they knew they were pregnant, I knew. I could see it in their eyes somehow, and in the beginning I would make comments or ask if they were indeed pregnant. Most often, they didn't even know yet. Needless to say, for those who did not want to be pregnant, they began to approach me with the sign of the cross as if I were a vampire. I learned not to comment anymore as I was beginning to feel like the grim reaper of motherhood.

There was another negative side effect developing. I usually saw the best in people--the most they could possibly hope to be. While this effect was generally positive, I could also sometimes see the darker side if it was so dark that it proved dangerous for me. This clouded my judgment for years and sent me into "fix it" mode with many people. While I hoped for their best and most confident selves to come shining through, at times my hope exceeded their own desire to bring forth these same traits. I remained in this mode for many years. The result was that I put myself in abusive positions, and I wasted far too much time with people who were not then, and may never be, on a journey to seek out their highest spiritual abilities and best selves. For one on this journey, that type of expended energy is almost the kiss of death. It made me sad, tired, ill and despondent when I was around people content to be their most mediocre spiritual selves. I wasted too many years in this state, always seeking the good I saw in these people who were not ready to aspire to achieve it..

I still want the best in all people to shine through, but now I pray to the one who can help that happen. I strive to keep my miniscule ego out of the situation and focus my thinking that I can actually facilitate such support and changes on a physical plane. I know at all times that all changes and abilities come only through the grace of God and each of our own efforts to match the lessons She has put in front of us. Another person can pray for us, but they can't will us to grow spiritually.

Spiritual growth is a natural state of being. In order to avoid growth, you have to force yourself to do so. We do this by first and foremost believing that we actually run our own lives. We then exercise our free will to force situations to move at the pace that we determine they should so that we can remain safe. Unfortunately, we have to engage fear and ego for this to occur. At that point, we are out of synch with God's plan for us and the directives for this lifetime that we came here in spirit form to accomplish. By forcing our own agenda, we ensure that we cannot effectively accomplish God's agenda for us. If we free flowed with God's plan, we would move at the speed of sound.

Let me give you an example: Early in my direct communication with God, I was told that I need to master a foreign language beginning with Arabic. God was perfectly willing to teach me, and began speaking Arabic to me during the course of the day. After about two days of this, I couldn't handle it. I don't know why, maybe I thought I needed to see it written, but there was something disconcerting about having Arabic piped into my head without warning. I purchased some language tapes and was much more comfortable.

How ridiculous, but I slowed my progress by thinking I needed to do this at my own pace--not God's. I forced myself into some form of rejection, and therefore could not comprehend the information coming in. I convinced myself that it was too fast, and therefore, it was. But the truth is, God is way smarter than I am. If I had said that it was too fast, I'm sure She would have adjusted. Even more importantly, if I had let my mind "loose" from my self imposed constraints, and not tried to run things, I'd probably be fluent in Arabic now. But instead, I put these restrictions on myself. Of course, since life is school at our own pace in part, God let me. I intend to break this tendency, but I have not fully succeeded yet in all areas.

This insistence on our own plan forces us into a nonsensical loop of repetitive behavior. The only escape is to let go and let God run this show so we can learn effectively because It is better qualified, but sometimes we just can't seem to do that. This is where faith comes in again. We must trust that we are not equipped to run things, and while most of us have a lot of evidence to substantiate that fact, still we don't let go. In my case, I kept trying to keep to the directives of my upbringing-- especially those from my father. His concept dictated that a man runs everything and women should only follow. However, I being his child and borne of his massive ego, felt I was capable of doing anything I wanted—as long as my husband said it was okay.

This massive dose of spiritual madness kept me reeling around in circles through three very wrong husbands, a dozen other really bad relationships, and for a good twenty some years. Given the fact that I wasn't prone to publicize my 'other world' life that I was experiencing, and my natural suppression of anything that made me look crazy (like all the other women in my family who I learned later also heard other/side folks), I was not developing my skills of communication with continued spirits. Quite sadly these skills went somewhat dormant for a time.

I lived in suppress mode, which among other things, turned on me and gave me an assortment of health problems for many of those years. Finally, when it was obvious that the last husband was delivering lessons that I just wasn't getting, I decided to divorce him. I finally learned that if I was too stupid to move forward and get these massive lessons that kept coming my way in too similar fashion, I would just take a break, look at all of these folks from a distance, learn some new working skills and see what happened. It took me about 7 years to sort out that that portion of the nonsense my father had taught me in my youth (he did have many great lessons too) was clearly not in keeping with God's direction and directives. I also began to understand my fear caused by trying not to be crazy. Once I was clearer, God had a chance to quite actively step back in with my training again without the interference of me being in the way. And step in She did.

CHAPTER FIVE
GETTING A HANDLE ON IT!

During my thirties, public contact began to make me ill—and still does today though I've learned how to handle it in most cases. Even prior to my thirties, spanning from my adolescence to my early twenties, I heard names uttered aloud. In the movie "What Women Want" with Mel Gibson and Linda Hunt, there is a scene when he first learns to hear what women think while he is walking through a park and can hear many women at the same time. Before I learned control of the voices, I could be in a particularly open mode, and I would hear names from all the people in a crowded room, much like him in that scene.

This ability became incredibly difficult for me. In my early twenties I took on a job with 90% public contact, and I had to virtually shut everything down in order to retain my sanity. If I heard a name when I was in contact with a live person, I ignored it. But even though I refused to listen, I became increasingly more sensitive and people's negative thoughts or problems began to affect me. Too much public contact began to make me physically ill. I also became supersensitive to the toxins that people wear, chemicals in food, in the air, etc.

By the time I left my third husband, I also left the job that was causing me so many problems. Still I didn't understand that my reaction to him was more spiritual than physical because he fought growth, tooth and nail. My environment was making me ill because of the level of spiritual chaos that he and the job were inducing, or in which I allowed myself to participate.

In my late thirties, I had to retrain for a more spiritual friendly job in which I had less contact with people, but nothing else was going quite right. Money was always a problem, contract work was very, very difficult for me, though I had no trouble getting work for everyone else I knew. Things just weren't right and were always difficult. Then I experienced a bizarre physical accident when I broke my collarbone by doing too many sit-ups. I am heavy-chested and was trying to lose the weight that just kept creeping up on me. I discovered it only takes less than 8 pounds of pressure to break the collarbone, and doing 500 and 600 sit ups a day with a tight sports bra on snapped it. Odd, but true.

One day I found myself with a broken collarbone, trying to talk to a saleswoman on the telephone about some services for my freelance business, rescheduling the appointment for the next day because of the doctor's appointment, and explaining why her serviceman could not wear cologne when he came out. She waited patiently until I finished and then said, "Honey you are having a very hard time aren't you?"

"It's been like this a few years now." I responded.

She said, "Dear, I'm a Christian woman, and sometimes Jesus lets me see things. May I tell you what I see?"

I had spent years listening to people who were crazy, and listening to people who talked about people being crazy. I thought I knew what insanity might sound like, and she was moving in that direction. I didn't want to be impolite and never actually imagined that there were people who had real control of the flashes I had experienced. Her words meant little at first, but I humored her.

"If you have some insight, I'd sure like to hear it." I replied.

"Baby you have a curse on you. A lot of negative energy that is affecting your life. Do you feel like you can't make anything happen the way it should, like you are just spinning your wheels and all kinds of things get in the way?"

I figured that it was a lucky guess, and not too hard of one at that since it was evident that everything around me was a bit off and wrong. She didn't have to be a genius or psychic to figure that out from our conversation. I was polite, and said thank you. Just as I was about to move back to the conversation about the business services, she asked, "Would you like for me to describe the woman who put this curse on you?"

My heart skipped a few beats, and I was quiet. So she repeated it. "Honey, do you want me to describe her? She really hates you and you might want to get a description so you can beware in case you know her. Shall I describe her?"

I sat down at my desk, shocked. "You can do that?" I asked.

"Sometimes, Jesus willing. Today I can." She answered.

"Then yes Ma'am." I said. "Please do."

She described the woman's skin complexion, height, weight, hair color and length, eyes – which were unusual, clothing style, color of her outfit, jewelry and facial expression. Then she asked if I knew the woman she'd described. There was no mistaking who she was. Her hair, eyes and clothing style were too distinct to be anyone else.

"That's my sister." I stammered.

She paused for a moment then said. "No, I don't think so dear, this woman really hates you and it has something to do with a man, twenty years ago. Let me pray some more and ask, because I just can't imagine that a sister could hate another sister this much. Let me pray, and I'll get back to you tomorrow."

She never got back to me. A technician made all the future calls. I called her once, and she had him return the call. I know now because I have asked, she didn't have the heart to tell me that my sister really did hate me that much, but I knew it was the truth as soon as she said it. In addition to this woman's warning,, I had been having some very strange things happen with dark shadows standing over my bed, and uncomfortable, ominous feelings in the dark that had come and gone, but had been more prominent for the past couple of years. Negative energy sent to a sensitive person can manifest itself in odd ways becoming quite frightening.

This was my first knowledgeable experience with a true clairvoyant. Before that, it had been hit and miss and mostly chaos while I tried to navigate the legacy of confusion that had become my mother's and my life. I had been hiding because I never thought this ability was controllable, so I avoided it. This woman was the first person I had seen who had full control of what was happening to her, and with one ten minute conversation or reading, she had changed my life. The cat was out of the bag, and I would have to catch it!

CHAPTER SIX
WHO YOU GONNA CALL?

Finding a ghost buster, curse breaker, or conjure person when you haven't a clue about how negative energy operates is no easy task! I had not put together enough information in my personal knowledge arsenal to fully comprehend what I should do. I had a very close girlfriend from the country that went ballistic when I told her because she had seen plenty of that type negativity going on her whole life. Oddly enough, I had probably seen more spirits than anyone I knew except for my mother, but still I didn't piece things together. At that point, I felt without fully knowing, that there was some errant energy causing all the ruckus in my life. So at the insistence of my friend, I set out to find someone who knew what to do about a curse.

When I began to ask around, I found I had a truly eclectic group of friends. One suggested a Hindu practitioner who began talking about how we would have to send the energy back to my sister and destroy her; another was a Christian minister who had banished all manner of negativity from an assortment of folks, but who was slightly arrogant in his approach to me; and the last was a Priestess of Ifa, a religion of the Yoruba people of Africa, who was kind and gentle, easy-going and approached the conversation suggesting the least amount of spiritual work to stop my sister, but not to hurt her. Needless to say, I chose her.

She was nothing like I expected. She was sweet, gentle, unassuming and felt like an older sister (like somebody else's older sister, at least not the one that was giving me trouble). She gave me a series of prayers to say, candles to light, things to do that all seemed harmless. I didn't see how they could stop a curse if it wanted to persist. She politely said it had nothing to do with us, but with the spirits on the other side and what they decided to do about it based upon what we asked. She also said that once I started doing these things, the person who was causing the problems would probably reveal themselves to me. She explained it would become uncomfortable for them and they would usually have to respond somehow, if only to fish to find out what I knew.

I diligently did everything she said.

I found out that the incident that caused the rift between my sister and I involved a man we'll call Clarence. At least that was what the Priestess thought. Twenty-five years before, I dated Clarence for about a year. He was a serious womanizer, and our dating relationship just sort of faded away. We remained friends, but I knew who he was.

Twenty five years before my talking with the clairvoyant, my sister was living on the opposite coast and my family had not been able to contact her for several months. We were worried, so I got on a plane and went to her house to report back to the family. Clarence, who was living in that city, picked me up from the airport and took me to my sister's house. I was married and my friendship with Clarence was quite platonic. Also, I was grateful that he had the time to help me find my sibling in an unfamiliar town. We found her apartment. She was having a very hard time. She had divorced her husband, lost her job and didn't want anyone to know. Our father—a divorcee himself-- had instilled in us an absurd attitude concerning divorce which basically dictated that it was always the woman's fault. By this point I'd learned to disregard this notion, and I certainly did not blame my sister, but she was worrying about everything and generally doing poorly.

At first she wouldn't even open the door of her apartment when I knocked and identified myself. Instead, she made us go to the corner coffee shop for 30 minutes while she got ready. When we got back we found her super thin, drawn and had on make-up that was way over the top with Nefertiti eyes, and two toned lipstick. There were dark candles around the room and a lot of black decorations – curtains, objects painted black that normally weren't, etc. It was somewhat surreal, and in the middle of that, she and Clarence started a weird flirtation that struck me like watching a runaway train, sure to wreck. I thought surely my eyes and ears were playing tricks on me because he apparently could not see what I saw going on with her and still feel prone to move in her direction and not expect some sort of drama. She was very dramatic.

When we got in the car, I asked him to refrain from doing what he normally did and go for the dog in him as this was my sister, and she was clearly having great difficulty. He promised he would not get involved, but would watch out for her. He took me to the airport, I got on a plane, went back to my family, called my parents and filled them in. When I spoke with my sister again, I cautioned her about getting involved with Clarence as he had no scruples about women. She informed me she was grown and didn't need my mothering. I stayed out of it, hoping that Clarence would act honorably. Wrong.

They started a relationship that lasted about a month. One day she called and cussed me out because she decided that my jealousy of her caused me to do something to stop Clarence from seeing her. I tried to tell her there was no truth to that, but she wouldn't listen and became very abusive, which has often been her way. Our relationship went from distant, to annoyed on my part and cold on her part, to not much of anything. We had never been very close, but it moved to no communication over the years--or so I thought until the day the clairvoyant told me otherwise.

Therefore in 1997, when the clairvoyant told me about the curse, everything clicked into place and made some bizarre sense. We'd experienced some other minor tiffs during the 20 years, but the clairvoyant's interpretation certainly made sense. My sister was not honest in those days and would play games rather than trying to talk things out and get over them. She liked holding grudges.

Everything happened just like the Priestess said. One night my sister called, after not talking to each other for two years, and wanted to know what I'd been doing; how I was making a living; how my son was doing, and a few other things. It was strange. I'd been told to give her very little information, which I tried and accomplished, but she was relentless. Somewhere in that conversation she got angry with my avoidance and called me a liar. Suddenly, all the preserved venom that must have been in her heart for all those years came out. She threatened me and let me know that she was superior, that she would continue to make sure that only negativity came over my life, and that she was in total control of every ugly thing that came my way. It was hateful, venomous and way over the top.

Without going through too many details, that phone call sent me down a road of séances, revelations, readings and an array of tasks to be completed over the next two years in order to break what was a bonafide, generational family curse, which I never imagined was possible before. Now I know that concentrated energy can do all manner of things. It turns out my sister had been used by one of those real demonic spirits, not just a hologram, operating from the other side to disrupt our family lineage, and this had gone on since the mid 19th century. Another sister and I did everything we were told in order to break the cycle, and with the last act, which was break an object over the casket of a family member, (you can't imagine how hilarious, absurd, and strange that got while we were conflicted with social mores and desperation to have the madness end, as well as odd, Keystone Cop logistics) we could feel the energy change in almost every family member, including the odd sister. About three years later, she was almost unrecognizable as a person with the prior bad behavior; however, there was more before it got better.

CHAPTER SEVEN
HASTENED LESSONS

After the prayers and candles, the situation didn't change quickly enough. My son and I were getting small visitations at night by something that we couldn't identify. Whatever was driving my sister was persistent. The Priestess determined that we needed to execute a ceremony to find out the exact conditions of our generational curse. So we performed a séance of sorts, and mediums talked to my ancestors who gave us the crux of the matter and what had to be done. They also identified me as having similar abilities to them, and they plotted a course of action that ended almost two years later with that casket. After many ceremonies that I never would have believed I would be doing in life, we were told that the curse was broken. There is much here that I have been told not to discuss, so I must honor that. What is more important is that my odd sister became far less odd, stopped her threats and became almost downright sweet over the next few years, with none of the absurdities and meanness of the years before. It was certainly wonderful to see her behaving so differently.

This long drawn out, incredible incident convinced me that I really did need to know what I could do to better develop my spiritual side and abilities because these women, the Priestess and the two mediums she employed to help us, had a handle on a lot of information that I knew nothing about. I beefed up my reading and spent as much time in prayer by the water as possible. Then one day I picked up the pendulum dowsing crystal that a friend had given me, read the directions and began a whole new adventure.

For a person just beginning their spiritual lessons, the pendulum and divining in that manner provide tangible, physical evidence that you are speaking with a continued spirit, or someone not in this dimension. This process is not a hoax, as many nonbelievers think, though I have seen people who have not enough connection to the spirit world simulate results by swinging the pendulum themselves. That's not what we are talking about here. I'm talking about consistent evidence that someone else is speaking through the device.

For me, the pendulum was a training tool, used to help me learn to connect to the spirit world at will. At first I just asked generally what was happening, almost like a game. But if you are paying attention, you begin to notice the answers and the manner in which they come begin to change. Sometimes you are in the way, and at other times they (spirits) seem to be in the way. But, in the beginning of my lessons I started to understand that there are many factors that determine how the communication operates between us and the spirit world.

Through the differing responses on the pendulum, I learned that I was not always talking to the same people and had to develop different interviewing and questioning skills in order to get the most detailed answers from each person/spirit. It became a fascinating and addictive experience. The more I attempted communication, the easier the process. Then one day I noticed that every time I asked about a particular man I was involved with, the answers got more convoluted and confused. There are three positions on the pendulum. In my case, (and it is different for each pendulum) my pendulum swung to the left for no, to the right for yes and around in a circle for maybe.

Just before this, I met a new man while on business, a thousand miles from home. We hit it off almost immediately. I knew something was up when during our first conversation which should have lasted a few minutes, seven hours later he mentioned that at a desperate moment when he considered suicide, his Guardian Angel, all dressed in white, kept him from throwing himself onto the third rail of a commuter train. Yet when he looked over his shoulder again for her, she was gone. Almost every answer on the pendulum about the new man, whom we will call Kiljoy, was a maybe, or it might not move at all. All of this was odd considering how clear and concise the answers were about everyone else. Every once in a while the pendulum would not move at all. I figured out that something was wrong about the same time that one of my ancestor spirits got through and told me that all of my deceased family spirits, with whom I was now speaking at the beginning of my practice on the pendulum, were having trouble getting through to me because this errant spirit was interfering. This was all through a series of suggestions that I was beginning to hear more clearly in single words or partial phrases.

As I pieced things together, I was sent by my great grandmother to the computer to look up a massacre that occurred in the mid 1800's in the Caribbean. She also gave me the name Drake Parker (P.D. from chapter three). After a couple of days of research on the computer, I found a massacre that occurred because the British Governor allowed the British citizens in the predominantly black country to abuse the rights of the natives after they colonized the country. They ended up killing nearly a whole town of people though one of its most powerful citizens escaped. That man commanded a large group of islanders and they stormed a courthouse, locked all the Brits inside and burned it and the neighboring houses to the ground, killing many Brits. It was a major incident that transformed the country.

I learned later that Parker Drake was a British woman who died in that fire, along with her four children, husband, sister, mother and father. Kiljoy was a direct descendent of the man who led the raid, and when I saw a picture of him, he looked almost exactly like Kiljoy. I went back to my pendulum and called Parker by name. She answered. Over the next week and many questions later, I learned that she had put a curse on Kiljoy's family line. Except it was not stray energy that she submitted for their destruction, she was actively engaged in causing them much confusion and discomfort, and apparently she had done so very effectively.

Kiljoy had a series of odd and unusual health problems, and as I learned more about him, I found out that he was an incredible liar, mean, confused, and ultra combative. He was also one of the most incredibly chauvinistic men I have ever met. This was part of the curse as well, I learned from Parker.

I started out conversing with the spirit, Parker, because she had taken to blocking all other spirits from speaking to me or would step in the moment I asked about Kiljoy. She would give me accurate information about anyone or anything else I asked about, but the moment I asked about anything related to him, she would lie, mislead me and make an array of problems till I finally figured out that it was her. Stupidly, on my part, I tried to make it clear that she could not win, and that I was there to stay, which turned out not to be true, but it was my best game at the time. She laughed at that and reminded me that she had been around for over 150 years, and who did I think I was.

Acknowledging that my approach was faulty (go figure), I began to try and get to know her.

I found out that she and one son who had held the grudge with her were in the same place in the spirit world, but that the rest of her family was in another place that she knew to be more pleasant, away from them. That's when I began to understand the different levels of the continued spirit activity. She said that she was not in what we might call hell, but that she and her son were not allowed to leave, whereas people in the more free side could travel openly. There were other people with her, but they didn't seem to have much to do with each other. In her location there was almost nothing to do but wallow in their hatred of whomever they had decided to affect. It was a choice she had made, and she was not letting go of it because she wanted all of Kiljoy's family to suffer for the duration, and she was sticking to it.

It was a rough couple of months because she spent most of her time trying to make me think all sorts of horrible things about Kiljoy, including that he was a child molester, had been molested by a parent, was a murderer and the list went on and on. I nearly thought I was losing my mind half the time because she made great arguments and cases for most of her lies, and supported them with examples or possibilities. Other strange things started happening also. For instance, out of the corner of my eye I could see things moving in the house, and I was hearing an array of sounds that didn't seem human. I thought I was going the route of my female relatives.

I struggled for my sanity, but every once in a while, one of my real ancestors, as Parker would pretend to be them too, would get through and encourage me to be strong and stick with the situation because it was, in part, a test. I have come to call this phase of communications "hazing" over the years, because it is much like hazing for a fraternity or sorority. A lot of drama and tests from spirits who vibrate at a lower frequency fall into this category. I know now, that a lot of schizophrenics never make it past this phase. Apparently, my mother stayed at that point much of her life.

I was trying to figure out whose test it might be, and who was administering it. I started to hear Parker and my ancestors more clearly. I began to see a friend who was a psychologist who was kind enough to meet with me once a month to make sure I was not really losing my mind. She determined that she didn't know what was happening to me, but that after many questions, I didn't appear to be crazy (my words, not hers). It was rough!

After several weeks of mass confusion and talking with Parker, and more evidence that my little weak "you won't win here" nonsense was not working and had only aggravated her more, I asked if she didn't miss her husband and other children. She said that she did, but that there was nothing she could do about it. I asked her why not? If she stopped her behavior, because God was a kind God, shouldn't she able to appeal to His patience and leniency? She said that she did not think so because she had done so many despicable things over time. I learned and felt the pain she had accumulated over the years, and how much more she had caused herself by sticking to her intended destruction of the Kiljoy line.

Just like those of us on this side get stuck, she was obviously stuck on a destructive hamster wheel herself. I suggested that she and I pray together every day and ask God to help her stop the meanness in her heart and allow her and her son to move to the place where the rest of her family was located. She said that the only reason the child spirit was with her was because he refused to leave her. It was a mess that she and Kiljoy certainly needed to be free of. So we prayed. She said that in over 150 years, and all the people she had wreaked havoc upon, I was the first and only person who had ever prayed for her. Many had prayed for the Kiljoy line, but none had prayed for her.

We prayed every day, sometimes two or three times a day, for about three, almost four months. Kiljoy's health began improving, but he was still crazy as a bed-bug and an incredible liar, and we stopped talking to one another after a couple of months. Still Parker and I prayed. As time went on, she became less venomous when she talked about his family, and from time to time, she would contact me and ask to pray. She said that she genuinely liked me, other than the fact that I cared for the evil Kiljoy.

Then one day she spoke to me while I was in the car and said that she had something to tell me. That was a new and developing skill because I was still using the pendulum to verify that I understood her, and we were nowhere near the pendulum. My listening abilities were changing, but I still used the pendulum to make sure, like a security blanket. She confirmed that she wanted to let me know that she and her son had been allowed to move to the side of their dimension where the rest of her family resided, and the change was brought about because I had worked in unison with her to pray and God had granted it. Of course, I thought it was just another trick, which she said she knew I would think, so she suggested that I speak with my Grandfather. He confirmed what she had said, and it appeared to actually be him. This is difficult to describe, but at these times, the clairsentience kicks in and I can feel truth and lies.

Within a couple of months, Kiljoy called and sounded much better though he was still reeling in some of his own madness from having lived his entire life under Parker's influence. He was lighter, though there was no hope of us working things out personally. Though the extent of his personality problems confused me at first, he was still a seriously damaged, controlling, man with horrible habits he had developed over his lifetime. He was not someone I wanted to know, curse or not. But I didn't want him dead, or in such physical or spiritual pain, so I was glad for Parker and the cessation of her attacks on his family.

At the beginning of my relationship with Kiljoy, I had received a reading from an Ifa practitioner who said that I was in Kiljoy's life to save his life, but that we might not make it further than that. This message sounded cryptic and crazy to me when I first heard it. But it became clear as a bell when I saw the difference after Parker let Kiljoy and his family go in order to move her own spirit life back in the light. It was a deeply important lesson for me about how we affect so many more than ourselves with all behaviors.

Since I had free access to the pendulum and was getting much more free flowing information in the form of phrases and words, I learned that all of my ancestors and supporters were elated with my progress. I was told that I had executed a huge task and had a big graduation. I had no idea what that really meant, until that day I was sitting on the porch . . . and I heard that which I never imagined I would.

CHAPTER EIGHT
GOD ON THE PORCH

I had taken my notepad and pendulum out to the screened porch to do my morning reading, a ritual I had been observing for almost a year. Parker had been back with her spirit folks for at least a month and contacted me often to thank me for helping her accomplish the change. She was sweet, light and wonderfully happy. I sat in a rattan chair, took the pendulum out of the case and prayed that my questions and answers be guided by the light of God. As I held the pendulum up, I heard a cacophony of multi-voices in my head, made up of what felt like several hundred voices in all tones, qualities, and ages speaking simultaneously to me. It said, "You don't need that anymore to hear."

I asked "Who are you?"

I heard, "I am what you would call God."

Well, I took off running down the steps and out into the yard, when it occurred to me that there was nowhere to run, and nowhere to hide. I thought about it for a minute and then walked back up on the porch and sat down. I heard, "Now that's more reasonable." I immediately broke into tears as if there was no choice whatsoever. I didn't mean to cry, I just didn't seem to be able to control my reaction. The voice waited patiently and said nothing. I concentrated and hoped it had gone away, as I was sure I had lost my mind.

I heard, "You have not lost your mind. I am your God. You have done well, and you have done what few in your situation might have chosen. You prayed for a spirit who meant you harm. Things will change now. You have graduated to a new level. Be glad." The voice was booming, and had too many levels and pitches for me to concentrate on the words but it sounded like the singing and speaking of hundreds of adults and children. I was trying to process what had been said as well as how I was hearing it. The voice said, "I will change the frequency so that you might absorb my voice better." By the end of that sentence, there was one male voice with an odd echo behind it.

I still wasn't glad because I was sure I was insane at that point. Because of conventional religious dogma, I rejected the idea completely that the one and only God that I knew might be talking to me. The voice responded, "But do believe it, I am that entity." The voice started out male, and by the end of that sentence, it was female.

I asked, "Are you male or female?" It answered, "I am neither and both. I am all things that you know of and all genders that you can conceive, and yet I am no gender but neutral." And the voice went back to male, about mid sentence. I responded by saying that I was having a hard time keeping up with the gender changes from beginning to the end of sentences. It responded, "What would you prefer?" I answered "Male." It said "Alright, for the moment. But you must get accustomed to both energies, and able to hear either and address either, as that is more appropriate." That made sense from a feminist stand point, however I wanted to hear something different enough from my own voice, to help me be sure I wasn't making it up.

I decided that though that helped, I still didn't know who was speaking. The explanation didn't make much sense to me either because I never expected to hear God actually speaking to me in the first place. I said that I wanted to ask the pendulum about the origin of the voice. Of course, It laughed and said go ahead. So I did. I identified that I was speaking with my Grandfather and asked him if that was actually God speaking to me. I saw the pendulum swing yes, and I could hear a man's voice say yes. I asked for my mother, who also said yes as the pendulum swung yes. It was the first time I could hear them completely, in full sentences and separate and distinct voices and not just phrases and thoughts mixed together. My mother said I should be glad that I was allowed this honor, and that I had done well.

I asked the God-voice, still not fully convinced that it was God, how I would know if It was not actually demonic and trying to make me crazy? It asked me if I had a plan to go crazy? Of course I said no, and It said then that wasn't really an issue then, was it? I said that I wanted to go back and ask the pendulum more questions. The God-voice said that it would no longer work for me because I didn't need it any longer. Of course, skeptic that I was, I tried it, and all it did was move around in circles.

That was the first day of my revelation. I left all of it alone and did not speak to anyone I couldn't see anymore until the next day, trying to see if I would be running down the street with my hair on fire I guess, mad as a hatter.

The next morning, I tried talking to my more familiar folks, ancestors and the like, through the pendulum. It didn't move at all. The God-voice said "It will no longer work for you. You do not need it. It's time to move on." I put the pendulum down, but I also didn't fully believe that it was God I was speaking to, so I didn't talk that day to anyone else. God is incredibly patient.

The third day, I picked up the pendulum and I heard the voice again say, "You are not listening. It will no longer work for you. You must move on to the next phase. There is nothing to be afraid of." Being stubborn and hardheaded (conditions we will discuss more later and how they retard growth), I held the pendulum up and asked it if it would answer my questions, as I had done many mornings. I had chosen to ignore whoever that was talking to me. The pendulum swung to the highest point on the left side, which indicated no, and hung there, defying gravity for about two seconds before I threw it down and ran out of the house and back into the yard again. Don't ask me where I thought I was going. I didn't say I was getting brighter, just more rattled. I stood there for a moment before I realized that lightning wasn't going to strike the house, as if it couldn't find me in the yard--not processing well apparently.

I slowly started up the stairs to the porch when I heard the voice say, "Have you had enough yet?" I sat on the porch and tears filled my eyes. The only thing I can figure out is that this experience was so unexpected that I could not process what was happening. I answered, "I just don't believe that you are God. I think you might be a more powerful ghost like Parker, but this seems inconceivable." The only answer I got was that it was not. I calmed down and prayed to the real God who didn't actually talk to people, to protect me. There was no answer, just as it should have been!

The next few weeks were clearly designed as training for me. During this time, I progressed to the point that I met my Spirit Guide, an Inuit woman from the 15th century. I had been introduced to my Guardian Angel during the family curse, but had only been able to hear her name before. I became able to hear all of my ancestors fully in complete sentences, and I could hear God completely. Over the course of a year, I learned to communicate with the Saints, Angels, and Orisha. But before I got comfortable that it was really happening, I found myself testing God, a lot. I guess She/He humored me, but once, I got defiant and went way too far. I ran up against what I refer to as my "Obedience Lesson"!

As I have said, my life is annoyingly annoying. Though not horribly hard it is filled with constant aggravation. Again I'm told I need to build spiritual character and stamina for whatever is coming my way. On the day of writing this, I was driving to a city about two hours away on business in 40 degree weather at 7:30 a.m. when I realized that the heat stopped working. With cold feet and hands, I made it to my destination. On the drive back, about 30 miles outside of my home, the window on the driver's side next to my head, exploded and all the glass shattered while I was doing about 75 mph on the highway. It sounded like someone had shot through the window. I wasn't hurt other than a little glass in my hair, and what felt like a tiny piece that must have grazed my eye. I pulled over, brushed away some of the glass, and got back on the highway.

God and I were having a conversation about something else at the time. I asked why She/He had not warned me that it was coming. The answer was this. "That would defeat the purpose of your training. It is stamina and endurance you are building, and the patience and calm to handle anything. Look at how far you have come. Your heart rate didn't even rise." That was true. I've had so much of this kind of thing now that it barely affects me because I know my condition for learning is "constant aggravation", and that it is my lesson plan in part, to achieve these described directives. In fact, this is the second time that the glass in that particular car exploded. The first time occurred about two years earlier when I was driving down the highway and the front window exploded. On most days now, I barely flinch if this type of thing happens. But at the time of my introduction to direct communication with God, I was a kicking and screaming, complaining fool! That all stopped with a serious God demonstration.

My son and I were coming back from a rental house I owned in another city. We'd just completed a lot of work and were still having a hard time with more repairs. Everything had gone wrong. I was fighting with the city over issues; I was in the middle of a fight with the next door neighbor; and I had a very difficult tenant who was also a relative that I needed to evict because he hadn't paid rent in a year. I was still making payments on the house and couldn't do both, and I was fairly sick of the entire thing. My son had to be at work the next day so I was driving back at 4:00 a.m. with two hours left to drive. I drank coffee, which I can't do without getting gittery, and ate chocolate candy to stay awake. Neither of those things works well with my supersensitive system, but they normally just tended to make me nervous. God chimed in while I was driving and told me to stop doing the things I knew ultimately worked against me and to find more discipline. In my world, I am charged with the task of constantly finding energetic and/or spiritual ways to deal with things like this and not choose the negative material ways to handle things like lack of sleep.

I didn't say anything, but quietly, ignored Her/Him/It, like It couldn't hear my thoughts . . . right! During that time I still questioned who I was speaking with from time to time, and wasn't so sure that It wasn't something demonic. We arrived home at about six a.m., tired and though my son could sleep for a while, I needed to work. I fixed a cup of coffee, got one of the doughnuts I'd just grabbed on the way in, and sat at my desk. Just as I was about to bite into the doughnut, I heard, "Don't eat that. You are just being disobedient now. Stop yourself."

As I've said before, humans are arrogant and we believe that we have far more power than we do, just like any two year old, and that often leads us to do really stupid things. I'm no exception, which is why I guess I was given the task of writing this book. I know of which I speak when discussing human frailty or, in this case, downright stupidity. In that state, I said, "I'm not sure who you are because if you were God, I doubt that my life would be this continuous hell all the time considering that I do everything you say and act in the manner in which you have designated. So I think you must be something other than that and I reject this and you."

I heard, "However, be that as it may, I am telling you now to get a hold of yourself, and not to put that in your mouth. You are just being self-destructive because you are frustrated, and that is not allowed for you. Put it down." I said something really, really dumb like "humph", and took a bite of the doughnut and was about to drink a sip of coffee, but didn't get that far. Immediately, my skin was on fire and a layer of hives rose up about an inch all over my body. I mean on every inch –

hairline, face, legs, neck, hands, arms, stomach, thighs you name it. It was horrible and looked and felt like I had a new strain of measles because it itched so badly, but along with the itching was a burning that felt like I had put my hand in a blazing, roaring fire. I threw the doughnut in the trash, and put the coffee down, but even that much movement was too painful. I could see the hives and welts sitting high on my skin and knew that this was not a reaction to doughnuts, but something quite intentional, and something beyond my doing or control.

I sat like that for about five minutes afraid of what was next, but nothing new happened. The intensity was severe and stayed that way. I managed to get up and make it to the bathroom and looked in the mirror. I looked crazed and my face was red and looked just like it felt, on fire! I hobbled back to my office in tears, careful not to rub any part of my body against another part, arms held out away from my sides. I sat down and waited. I called out to God, but got no answer. This went on for about ten full minutes, possibly the most terrifying moments in my life. I fully expected my head to spin around or to be levitated from the floor. It just looked like more proof of something demonic to me, but I wasn't going to think that too loudly and definitely would not say it.

I heard Him say "Now do I have your attention?" I said, "Yes Sir." Like the suddenly obedient child I should have been initially.

"Good. Now listen carefully. Yours is not a journey like you have seen before for all the reasons I have explained over the past few months, directly and through your spirit guides. You are not allowed to be disobedient and you are not allowed tantrums. You must develop patience, which you lack, and a calm spirit. And you must be disciplined. You know who I am whether you like it or not, and I have been clear with you about that. You know I am not demonic, and you must understand now, that you are never to refer to me that way again. Do you understand?"

I said, "Yes Mam, but this kind of action does make a person wonder."

Since that time, I might get a laugh out of God for a statement like that, in a time like that – of which fortunately there have been no more that severe. That day, there was no laughter.

"I could see that, but this is not a thing for you to wonder about. You must be clear that I am what you would call God, and not what you would call Satan, and you must treat me accordingly and not with such disrespect. Do you understand? Have I asked you to do anything that was bad for you, or would do harm to any other being?"

I answered no, which was true.

"Have I asked you to do anything that ultimately would not be good for you?"

I answered that I could think of nothing wrong with the requests and that they were ultimately for my own good. "Alright then. You are not to speak to me with such disrespect anymore, understand?"

"Yes Sir. I do. I will not do this again." I answered.

"Good. Now I know you are frustrated as yours is a frustrating life, but you must trust that I have reasons for this and follow my guidance. Do you understand?" He said.

Of course I might have said anything at that point if I thought I could get away with it, but I was more afraid of the consequences of a lie than the state I was in at that moment to even think in those terms, so I told the truth. Whatever might be happening, certainly, if I understood disrespect in that vain, was never going to happen again. I was through! Finished! Obedient as all get-out and just hoped I was siding up with the right entity.

"Yes Mam, I do understand."

Within about a minute from my last statement, all of the hives went down and my skin was cool and normal again. I got up and went back to the bathroom mirror and looked. There was not a mark, a red place, or anything on my face and arms. I felt no heat or burning nor itching anywhere. I cried even harder, as during the conversation, I had calmed down some, but it all came back as I stood gazing in the mirror. I was beginning to calm down again when I heard God's voice call my name, quietly, and without any force whatsoever. Even during the height of the hives there was no volume, though I detected sternness. When I finally stopped crying, I heard Him speak.

"Now go to sleep. You are tired, frustrated and you don't have to work right now. It is inappropriate when you are so tired. Get in the bed and sleep." And I did, and slept for about six hours. When I awoke I felt great. The first question I asked out loud was if God was there. The answer was, "Always." That ended my temptation toward disobedience, and I had new respect for the journey and my primary guide.

CHAPTER NINE
THE AUTOMATIC TENNIS BALL SERVER

I've been asked what it takes to hear continued spirits. I am still learning on a daily basis so there are concepts that have expanded from my first experiences, but there are some basic theories. It's impossible to hear the other side if you are busy with your own thoughts overtaking the communication channel. One cannot have free communication on any spiritual level if you have already decided that you know everything, or how it operates, or what you might, or should experience. Generally speaking, you don't know enough, and your spirit, mind and heart are not open enough for a new experience if you think you do. This will block the acquisition of new information. You must clear yourself and get out of your own way in order to be able to reach continued spirits, or even more importantly, for them to reach you.

Think of it as an automatic tennis ball server. You've seen those machines that professionals and trainers use to automatically serve the ball to a tennis player so that they become accustomed to executing the rapid return of balls coming from different directions. Think of the balls as your own thoughts and your own interference. You try and connect to the other side, or to God, and you end up thinking about the report card your child brought home from school, and how you will have to find him a tutor by the end of the week because you don't know enough upper level math to help him. Then you try and get the thought out of your mind because you are supposed to be praying, meditating or being still in your soul so that you can connect to God or your angels, or your mother or whomever. So you knock your thoughts aside and try and go still inside again, but another thought from your own mind gets in the way. You knock it aside, and another comes, and so on and so forth, until you get all the thoughts out of the way and your mind is still and quiet.

Since spirits and God (who uses any and all frequencies) use a lower or possibly different frequency to speak, I would recommend that you start there. Try and speak with someone with whom you were very close to and likely carry some of the same frequency. Shared DNA might help as there is physical DNA, but there is also in essence, spiritual DNA. From my understanding, we are all the same, but the closer our relatives are, the more succinct that range becomes. In other words, we are all spiritually, structurally very similar, like say in the range of 1 to 100 vibratory levels, but families may all fall within 45 to 65 range. That does not mean that we can't change the range to be higher or lower by our spiritual actions, however it is likely that we are more able to connect with those within our general range more readily. The higher your range, whether by spiritual genetics or hard work, the more able you are to connect with a broader range of spirits. So a person operating on an 85 will most likely be able to communicate with a wider variety of frequencies than a 30 frequency person, unless they work at raising their frequency.

Given this theory, if you first pray to God for guidance and ability to connect to your loved ones who have continued on, and then concentrate on communicating with them, you are more likely to be able to reach family than others initially. Next, you must clear all of the thoughts coming at you, or that you are developing, like the tennis balls from an automatic machine. Depending upon your concentration level, training and natural tendency to clear your mind, with effort and time you should be able to keep batting the interfering thoughts away until there are no more left, and your mind and spirit grow silent. At that point, continued spirits can get through.

When the thoughts in your head have stopped (and it might take years to learn to eliminate all errant thoughts and concentrate at this level) it becomes clearer when spirits are speaking, as their cadence, thoughts, concerns and demeanor are clearly not your own. You can tell the difference. Unfortunately, there are other continued folks who can come in as well, and not all are enlightened spirits. They look for an opening to communicate with this side and, once they find a person who can hear, they may interject their own agenda.

That is why it is essential that at all times, you begin any such efforts to communicate with a prayer that basically identifies who you want to guide this communication, and that is the Supreme Being of goodness and light. If guided by God, errant spirits generally cannot get through and interfere, unless it is part of God's lesson, and that does get tricky.

Otherwise you might think you are talking to your Aunt, and that could go on for months if you haven't prefaced your communications with the correct prayer. Then one day your aunt might tell you to do something that is just a bit wrong. Thinking it really is your aunt, you might be inclined to do it because of your history with her while she was alive. You knew her to be a very good woman, so you figure she must have good reasons for asking you do this, that you must not understand. You do what was asked, or it puts you into confusion and you toss away the entire process assuming that only evil comes from this type of communication.

It wasn't your aunt at all, because even though you opened the gate, you didn't open it to the right channel. You must open to the right channel and then errant spirits will not be able to get through. There is another trick too. It makes no sense, and I wouldn't believe it if someone told me, but I've experienced it so many times now that I know it is true. I've discovered that even misguided spirits won't lie to you repeatedly. The magic number for me anyway, seems to be four.

Usually you can feel that something is not quite right with the spirit with whom you are communicating when it is an errant or misguided spirit. Now bear in mind that they all have similar information, and access to much more. However, they, like us, process things through their spiritual level to some degree. They are also bound to stop at the points that the Creator demands they stop. What this means is that if we have a lesson to learn about something, and almost everything has to do with learning to connect to God, if an errant spirit's interference will help us to learn something then it is allowed. Especially if you did not ask for guidance and protection when you began this effort at communication, since that has a great deal to do with what we are all here to learn.

Open up correct communication with a prayer that goes something like this, "Dear Creator of light, wisdom, peace, tranquility, love, kindness, joy, patience, forgiveness, tolerance and abundance, I ask that you hear my humble attempt to speak to my relatives and ancestors who now reside in the spirit world. And that you oversee these communications and guide and direct me to walk closer to your brilliant light."

If you do not open up your communication correctly and God has decided that since you didn't see the need to do that, She might allow the interfering, errant spirit to play with your head for a while, until you figure out that the only way to stop it is to reconnect to God. Even then, God gives you a failsafe for true connection. For instance, if you do not open up your communication correctly, and that errant entity is pulling you down some just off your central path, if you begin to figure that out and ask this simple question. "Are you my Aunt Katie, or are you some other spirit meaning to interfere?" the first time the spirit will lie and say it is Aunt Katie. It will also lie the second time, but it will feel more wrong to you if you are operating at this frequency. The third time it will lie, but by the fourth time, the spirit will tell the truth. It is as if it can't hold in the farce any longer. This seems to be God's protection for us while we learn.

And what must we learn? Here's the gist of it: All things originate with God and must go through God to reach their highest good. One system of reaching the other side requires clearing one's head, and then attempting to reach the easier entities while making sure that you avoid the frequencies that vibrate on a lower level than you, as they are the easiest to reach at first. The higher frequencies are harder because you have to vibrate high enough to reach them. Misguided spirits operate lower and enlightened spirits operate higher. In my experience, these are the first keys to reaching continued spirits. They are spiritual concentration, elimination of interference, and always opening up the phone line with the right phone number, which is God's light.

CHAPTER TEN
THE $64,000 QUESTION!

Well here goes! The 64,000 dollar question that we all want to know, but have too much emotion and counter training built around for many of us to hear in a neutral manner, is who and what is God, and why are we here? The answer I have been given is not as glamorous as burning bushes, parting seas and other such communications. It is the reason I stayed in the closet so long, considering that people have started wars based on their beliefs of who God is and who we are in relation to the ultimate Creator and Divine Architect. The answer is too simple, and too dispassionate for most to deal with, but I've asked many questions surrounding this, in every manner I can think of to be sure I am hearing correctly, and here is the basic answer: (Believe or not)

God is an energy source more brilliant than our little minds can imagine. It/He/She is about the size of a Volkswagen, and is pure and unencumbered energy unlike any we know, and yet we are all part of that same energy. Our God, and yes, It is one of many – twelve to be exact – is the youngest of such entities. We reside in the youngest of the twelve universes, and our God has no active memory of how old the first universe might be because it occurred so far before Its time. It has knowledge of the other universes including the oldest, however it cannot express the time to me because I have no means to comprehend such a measure of time, and to some extent neither does It.

Our God is neither male, nor female, and yet possesses all genders, ages, races and other information in its being, as well as other humanoid species, non-humanoid peoples, creatures and beings from all solar systems within our universe. It also has a general knowledge of all of the species of the other universes. It is all things, and it can create or destroy all things that we know of.

Its sole purpose is to sustain, encourage, support and monitor a system of growth for all beings on this planet and all the rest within our universe for the primary purpose of developing and molding His new counterpart: the God of the thirteenth universe. That God will then create and design a new universe with new solar systems and start all over again to create Its counterpart. This is the manner in which life goes on in the universes – universal pro-creation. It is all quite simple, and yet infinitely complex. We are creatures in varying environments, in a race, sort of, for the position of "most enlightened", so that we might start our own universe. Each world has a different set of situations developed for growth, and we must find a way to rise to the highest level of those circumstances in order to stay in the game. However, instead of being in a race with each other, each of us is more in a race with ourselves, to achieve maximum growth. We should be ever trying to beat our own best game.

Earth is not the most primitive and certainly not the most advanced of the planets. We all have some knowledge of this when we arrive, which is how we develop the systems for thought that might assist us in becoming our best spiritual selves. They are clues. These varied systems such as religion, science fiction, meditation, astrology, physical exercise, mathematics, Yoga, Tai Chi, science and other practices that heighten our many types of awareness like telepathic abilities, self healing systems, etc., are all mechanisms to help us become our best selves when used correctly. All have equal importance, and none is more weighty than the other, but each is necessary to reach our highest selves and good. They are also the same systems that can bring us to our worst when used incorrectly. How we manage them is the key to the method and amount of progress we make.

Let me give you an example of how astrology might work with, not in opposition to, spirituality as I am coming to know it. If a Taurus, or a Scorpio wants to get a deeper level understanding of the areas of growth that are to be completed during this lifetime, astrology is a system of understanding that will help them figure out what areas they should work on. In the case of Taurus, they do have good points like tenacity, surefootedness, strong work ethic, that are probably helpful in growing out of their negative traits like stubbornness, singular vision and direction which makes them unable to see things that are evident in their lives. They should also focus on their inflexibility, their need to control; their ability to rearrange reality to suit what they want to do from time to time. This holds true for the other zodiac signs as well. Look at it as cheat sheets that God has made available for those who will seek. Consider astrology in the same manner you might religion and the Ten Commandments. God puts before us all the information that we need to accomplish the tasks of this lifetime. Our charge is to remain open minded enough to explore many things and not stay glued to one school of thought. Our job is to stay open-minded and flexible enough to take in the information without censoring before exposure and utilize what we can to continue to move forward. Stubbornness and short sightedness thwart growth. Thinking you already have THE answer will most assuredly prevent you from finding anything new.

We are imperfect beings and not too swift for the most part, so we are allowed many lifetimes to reach our highest selves. Many of us choose to level off, which is why I suppose we have no new universe. Many tools are used to encourage our growth, and we are not allowed to regress without being returned to spirit state. So we reincarnate, according to our need to grow, and we return to learn some form of the lessons neglected in the past. Life is school. We keep going until we get all the lessons, and we are allowed different skills each time to achieve lessons according to our expected path of growth.

Our primary purpose is to reach the highest level of awareness so that we, one of us, or perhaps a collective of us, can run the next show. After we do all the required work on this plane, whether one incarnation at a time, or several particle incarnations simultaneously, we may then go on to other planets if needed for our personal development. We go do more work on the next plane, dimension, as continued spirits, and so on, and apparently there are almost endless levels of this, until we have done all the work needed there. In other words, if you can see and touch somebody on this plane, we are still in a primitive state, no matter how advanced we seem or want to perceive ourselves. Our most advanced earthling is in the equivalent of kindergarten!

In addition to our private journeys, I suspect, though I have not been able to get complete answers about this, we each hold a piece of a huge puzzle to larger universal issues. Unless we learn from one another, we will never have the entire puzzle put together that represents our highest spiritual selves. We are forced to learn from one another in order to get the entire picture if we are to "win" the race. Not learning to interact for the spiritual good of ourselves and others is like holding back a piece of a jigsaw puzzle, and thus the picture cannot be complete.

That is really the whole shebang as I understand it, but a complicated school this is, at least for our little meager minds.

CHAPTER ELEVEN
THE SYLLABUS

How do we get to determine what we come back to learn? This decision is primarily guided by our Creator, as is Her job, with input from spiritual guides and angels and others it seems, in conjunction with us during our stay as continued spirits in preparation for our return. It is not chronological, but geared toward our needs for growth. Because we are all different and learn at different rates of speed, beginning with lifetime number one, we develop unevenly, and totally different from one another. So the concept of Karma is a correct one, but it is not a repayment system for what one has done wrong in an earlier life as some folks seem to interpret it. Karma is a lesson plan for subjects neglected that need to be attended to in future classroom sessions.

Think of each visit to earth (or whatever planet body to which we are sent) as a classroom session. Perhaps the training is more like a course than a grade because there are so many more levels than I originally imagined (remember we are barely in kindergarten at our most enlightened). We must do the work to pass the course first, then the grade, and then the level of study. In other words, we must complete math, social studies, PE, etc. first semester, just to get to the second semester. Each lifetime might be equivalent to a week in one subject class. Puts an out of control ego in check really quickly when you think about it!

Let's say that you came here and blew it during an early incarnation by killing someone out of greed. That happened in lifetime number 6. It does not mean that you revisit that mistake, or retake that class in lifetime number 7. What it means is that for whatever reason you didn't get the message that killing for greed would not help you be your best spiritual self, God will make a plan to help you understand that when She feels it is time to make the most impact on your comprehension of that lesson. That might mean that you don't revisit this lesson until lifetime number 46. If you have learned this in some other manner by then, you might not ever meet what people think of as Karma and have to deal with this again. God is not vengeful and does not make you "pay." He is a teacher who helps you learn.

A perfect example of this happened to a family I knew, through a chain of events in 2003. The son of this family was in his early 30's, was attending school, upstanding, and generally wonderful. He and a friend were at a party one night and met two young women who asked for a ride home. They took them to their home in a rather rough neighborhood. One of the women said she had to go inside to get something and asked the young men to wait. Feeling no danger, they did so. Three other young men came out to the car and, without warning, shot the son of the family and were trying to shoot the friend when he jumped out of the car and took off running. The first young man died.

This seemed like such a waste so of course, I went to prayer and asked why this had happened to such a reasonable young man. I was told that it was because in a past life, not the immediately prior one, but one a few lifetimes before, he had killed a man because he wanted his wife, and that he had adversely affected the man's children and didn't seem to fully understand that. This incident, his violent death, was the only manner in which this young man could see why doing so had not allowed him to become his best and highest spirit being. This seemed confusing because he himself had no children and so the lesson seemed a bit convoluted . . . or so we thought.

At the wake a couple of days later, one of his old girlfriends showed up with a 10 year old in tow, saying that she wanted her son to see his father before he was buried. The young man's mother was in shock! She remembered the mother of the child as being an old girlfriend, but had not seen her in years. The young woman said that when she got pregnant, they decided not to marry, and he knew that his mother would not approve so he never told her about his son. Generally, the deceased spent time with his son, supported him, but never let his family know he existed.

When they say that God works in mysterious ways, this is a perfect example of what is meant. The complexities of the lessons are incredible. Obviously everyone in this scenario had something to learn. The young man's mother may have been rigid and needed a lesson in flexibility; the child may have needed a lesson in recognition; the child's mother may have needed a lesson in maintaining secrecy or respect for other's opinions, or non-interference and on and on. God is a chemist who puts us together for reasons that we can't begin to understand, but always the ultimate purpose is our growth. How It goes about delivering those lessons is a matter beyond genius.

When I first came into this ability (for lack of a better way to put it), I asked any and everything that I could think of like a kid in a candy store. I finally realized I got many more answers than I actually wanted to know and learned pretty quickly not to ask so many questions. In one of my earliest sessions I remember asking God how She was able to handle so many issues from so many people, creatures, humanoids and animals on so many different planets and planes all at once. He said that He was connected to each of us with an energy beam that allowed Her to stay in touch with all beings continuously and that that was the easy part. In fact, It said that It would all be quite boring if we didn't have free will to keep everything so interesting, and that it was free will that kept Him engaged enough to stay creative in Her teaching. Which brings us to another issue . . . the choices we make.

CHAPTER TWELVE
WHAT'S BEHIND DOOR NUMBER THREE?

If you think in terms of each moment presenting choices and situations upon which we must make the wisest and best decisions possible, understanding all of these concepts becomes significantly easier. That is, it is easier if you buy into the concept that we are responsible every moment, of every day, for the decisions we make. We are responsible for the choices, but basically, God puts the choices before us, according to how we need to grow, and the plan that we and She jointly designed before our return to this plane.

For example, we have a situation that calls for a decision on our part, remembering that our purpose in life, simple as it is, is to reach our highest spiritual selves at all times. That means that we must make the decisions that best allow this process to happen. These decisions should operate out of love and not fear, and peace and joy and not hostility, greed and lack. So with every occurrence in life, God, being the interactive and living being that It is, puts choices before us that will force us to learn to make decisions that will allow us or prompt and push us toward being the most even-handed spirits we can be. Remember we are always in spirit form, whether surrounded by a human body or not. We are spirits on a journey toward enlightenment and growth, though we may exist in many material forms.

So, let's say we are faced with a situation, problem or dilemma. In considering this situation, we have three choices that can determine the possible outcome and our involvement with the results. The choices are, (figuratively speaking), behind doors number one, two and three. Door number one contains the most attractive choice. It allows us to pretty much continue in a comfortable mode, operating in a way that is familiar and gentle, at least for the moment. It doesn't require us to change very much, or do anything that we really don't want to do. It allows us to maintain status quo. We can do what we have always done before, with possibly only cosmetic changes, but no real in-depth changes.

Door number two requires that we experience some discomfort. We may have to break down some of our own beliefs and belief systems in order to make sure that we can execute the tasks required in order to make this choice. This is not always comfortable because we don't always like change, and usually we don't readily see the need for it or the reason we should have to do things that we don't find pleasant. Sometimes that can be as simple as not attending an event because we find the subject matter interesting but the delivery system--or lecturer boring. More than likely in our growth plan God has a reason that dictates we attend the lecture because he has something He wants us to hear. Often, we impose our own will and take the easy route, so we don't choose that door, opting instead for door number one because it is easier and has all the elements that we like.

Finally, there is door number three with its complicated and often distasteful elements. Sometimes we can tell that this option will promote growth, hence the phrase "that which does not kill me, makes me stronger." Other times, we don't recognize the growth potential and only see the discomfort. This is a tricky door because it can either be a warning, or it can be a gift to promote incredible, level shifting growth. It is very hard to tell which is behind door number three. Depending upon our make-up and what we came to this plane to learn, making this choice can be questionable, or incredible. However, the two things that will assist us are prayer and faith. We will talk about them later.

In our everyday endeavors, we have to choose each door on a moment-by-moment basis. If we choose wisely, we continue to grow at a steady pace. If we allow ego, fear, or stubbornness to guide our choices, we are likely to be comfortable for a while, and maybe even this entire lifetime, but not likely to make the best growth pace.

Let's say that you always choose easy door number one. You never choose door number three with its potential problems, and you avoid door number two as much as possible. Generally, though you may choose only door number one, God is likely to occasionally force door number two or three upon you in order to assist your growth. But it is our job to choose growth, not His to force it upon us as a constant mode of operation. She will use it occasionally just to shake things up so that we can keep moving. She will not; however, do our growing for us. That is our responsibility.

If you are a person who always chooses door number one over and over again, you are very likely to be back here on this plane again, and soon I might add, with much more difficult lessons that don't have the same easy comfort level as the one you are living now. Therein lies the danger of always doing what is safe, what is full of creature comfort, what makes you happy. If you have a situation come your way in different forms and each time you choose to take the route that will make you feel most comfortable, you are very likely missing the point of the lesson. God is trying to give you opportunities to make slightly more challenging choices that will allow you to grow and learn, not just stay comfortable.

My recommendation is to pick the hard route as often as you can, unless you just happen to like repeating subjects in school. When you choose the harder route, you improve your chances for growth. However, you must be careful to discern between stupid and difficult choices. Stupid choices usually look like they have some material benefit; difficult ones almost always look like spiritual growth is the only factor that might be beneficial. Difficult choices usually do not look like fun, but more like duty or work, and they almost always challenge the way you think which can be uncomfortable, but promotes growth.

Another example: Sometimes a person appears to be leading a seemingly charmed life. Things happen in almost fairytale fashion and they foolishly begin to think that they actually had something to do with it. They may be greedy, or selfish and nothing seems to happen but good. This may confuse people who are watching, as well as them, into believing that life is all a farce and that being your best spiritual self has nothing to do with where we are supposed to go. This is a very, very difficult distinction to make if you have been raised in a culture that believes that good begets good, and that evil begets evil. Nothing could be further from the truth, and yet it is true in some major sense of the concept. If we can learn this lesson, half the battle is won and we can make decisions based upon our effort to achieve maximum spiritual growth each lifetime. However, it is no easy lesson, and most religious systems work against any real understanding of this. It is an advanced concept, and not one for the fainthearted. But if you get it, the spiritual rewards are monumental.

CHAPTER THIRTEEN
THE ROLE OF GOOD AND EVIL

Without doubt, the role of good and evil is a volatile and misunderstood subject. Please remember that what I am writing is a compilation of my understanding of discussions with God and other spirits. In an ultimate sort of way, good is the mechanism we use to become our best spiritual selves. However, it is also subjective which is why so many religions exploit the concept in order to further their own agenda. Good, according to one culture, is not the same as another culture, so it may be difficult to discern the usage of this term. The same goes for evil. Therefore, clearly the terms and their usage cannot be used in an ultimate sort of way to describe an ultimate state of being, like being our highest or best spiritual selves. That state requires a compilation of activities and not a simplistic term or concept such as these. However, they are tools to help us get to this state, but only tools and not the goal.

Even writing this feels like writing a riddle, and I know what I'm talking about, so I can imagine how difficult a concept this is from someone else's perspective. There are many factors that relate to this.

For lack of a better manner in which to evaluate these ideas, the Webster's New World Dictionary of the American Language – College Edition; 1953 definition might be a good place to start. It is important to note that it does not give examples of what it defines as evil, like in sentence usage. It defines evil as follows:

" adjective - 1. Morally bad or wrong; wicked; depraved. 2. causing pain or trouble; harmful; injurious. 3. threatening or bringing misfortune; unlucky,; disastrous; unfortunate, as, and evil hour. 4. resulting from or based on conduct regarded as immoral; as, an evil reputation. Noun – 1. anything morally bad or wrong; wickedness; depravity, sin. 2. anything that causes harm, pain, misery, disaster, etc."

While all of these definitions have some validity, they are based upon subjective reasoning, supported by cultural biases for the most part. However, there is a definition that stands the universal test and applies to any culture or method of thinking that I believe should be applied to our understanding of this concept. Bear in mind that of all the talks I have had with God and continued spirits, they do not use the term evil, unless they determine that I cannot comprehend what is being said otherwise. Even then, it comes out something like "what you might think of as evil." In fact, that terminology was only used in the beginning of my communications. Now that I no longer think that way, they no longer have to communicate with me in such simplistic terms. Their choice for some spirit gone awry is to say that they are "misguided." Usually I try to use that term as well, but will use both for these purposes.

If we have a misguided spirit, in this life or on another plane, they always have one thing in common. These misguided spirits always execute some form of action that seeks to impose their will over another's rights. This imposition may occur with another person, group of people or creatures or objects in our plane, and sometimes in the next. Anyone who suppresses another's rights can be evil even if that person is not attempting to, in fact, exact misguided behavior upon them. That, to me, is the true definition of evil. Morality and all the other systems Webster uses to define evil fall under this larger action.

Most evil, of misguided behavior is difficult to comprehend and hard to identify if you are not an independent thinker. People who operate in evil seldom do so intentionally and rarely recognize the detriment of their actions. M. Scott Peck in his book "People of the Lie" best explains the concept and state of evil in everyday people. Evil does not always look like something demonic (obvious folks such as Hitler, Idi Amin, and Jeffrey Dahmer). It can also manifest itself in the will of a husband to control his wife's actions, or the will of a parent to protect a child by giving them fabricated information like "if you tell a lie, a monster is going to wait until you go to sleep and come out from the closet and eat your toes."

These actions build fear and take away another's right to connect to God and be their best spiritual self, because (in the case of the child) they are too busy trying not to be eaten alive, either by real or imaginary monsters. The evil occurs in the creation of the fear and the resulting immobilization of the spirit that occurs as a result. Let me say that again, because I think that people miss this point, from some of the discussions I hear of this. It is the act of instilling and creating fear, self doubt, confusion, hate, self loathing and a host of other negative things in another person, or callously causing them to feel those things for themselves or another person, which constitutes ***true evil***. Most true evil is very subtle and almost unrecognizable if you aren't paying attention. I'm sure that parent has no concept that their story of the toe eating monster could possibly have an evil effect on their child. But the residual terror can be long lasting and thwart the development of a normally developing spiritual being, if nothing it done to counteract this. The fact that they did not think this through completely, makes them err on the side of evil. They cared more about the result, than the development of the spirit of that child. This scenario actually represents a part of the tests that God puts before the parent and the child.

For instance, the choice to choose door number one – the lazy choice on the parent's part (tell a ridiculous lie that will stop all undesired action so perhaps the parent can sleep); and/or struggling to believe (the easy choice and door number one for the child) or not believe (the hard choice and door number three for the child) this absurdity as a five year old is the joint test. The spirit who makes the most difficult choice, is probably going to make the most spiritual progress. This is true for both the child and each parent, because one of the two parents probably made the choice to follow the other's lead.

We all make our spiritual journey alone to some degree, even when we are together as humans. However, without doubt, to utter such words and impose fear upon another being (even out of fear for their children's safety) is evil/misguided because its dishonesty promotes fear, and fear is self perpetuating. It takes on a life of its own after a while, and needs no new encouragement to branch out into other activities, thoughts, and decisions in a life, so its best not to introduce it intentionally and unnecessarily, or early. From what I've been told, the goal of this exercise is to overcome the evil and choose to be your best spiritual self always. In that manner, neither good nor evil is the ultimate goal, but only the mechanism to achieve the ultimate goal, which is spiritual growth.

Tragically, wholesale misguided behavior has become such a regular occurrence that we no longer recognize it if we are not clear about our connection to God and our purpose here. Again, that is the problem with this kind of true evil. It seldom makes a lot of noise, but instead, is very subtle, soft, imperceptible and looks quite innocent.

Don't believe it. It is the worst kind, and makes more people afraid, and agree to absurd behaviors, policies, systems and abuses of humankind because they cannot see it clearly. It is the primary mechanism for the "sheep" mentality. Create fear in subtle ways and you can make sheep do anything without thought or rebellion.

For example, the following is the definition of evil found in the Encarta World English Dictionary; 1999:

"ADJ.. - 1. morally bad – profoundly immoral or wrong. 2. harmful – deliberately causing great harm, pain, or upset as in "This evil act is clearly the work of terrorists." 3. Devilish – connected with the Devil or other powerful destructive forces as in evil spirits. 4. causing misfortune – characterized by, bringing, or signifying bad luck as in an evil omen 5. malicious – characterized by a desire to cause hurt or harm – an evil mood 6. disagreeable – very unpleasant – What an evil smell! NOUN 1. wickedness – the quality of being profoundly immoral or wrong 2. evil, Evil force causing harmful effects – the force held to bring about harmful, painful, or unpleasant events as in a struggle between good and evil.

What happened between 1953 and 1999? Why has a public information source decided to bias the thinking of the reader in this manner? Why didn't Webster do it before? What is happening here and who is seeking to influence whom in this situation? What door did the person who cleared the words "This evil act is clearly the work of terrorists" choose when presented with doors number one, two and three by God?

These reference materials were published in the United States. Presumably, they were created by citizens of the United States, or at least English-speaking people, and are primarily for U.S. distribution first and then foreign distribution. The United States has one of the worst track records of human rights violations of any country in the world against African Americans, Native Americans, Asian Americans and women. Native Americans have been killed off intentionally with "small pox blankets" and poisoned water supplies, hunted down and slaughtered en masse – men, women and children; African Americans have been enslaved, beaten, hanged, shot, sprayed with water, bombed, slaughtered on slave ships, pregnant stomachs of black mothers slit open while they were still alive and hanged; and Asian Americans have been imprisoned, killed and degraded at will during the history of this country. With these atrocities in mind, is there anyone who thinks that this dictionary is alluding to US citizens when it refers to terrorists? Not hardly.

This is a clear example of choosing the seemingly easy door number one. Someone (or an editing committee) in Encarta decided that this not so subtle dissemination of biased information was appropriate. This decision subsequently influenced many minds that take in this data and supported popular thinking about who terrorists are – which at that time was foreign (from another country), usually a person of color, politically or religiously driven, and anti American or European. But what effect does this erroneous dissemination of information do to all those minds absorbing this information? The logical question becomes whether or not the word "terrorist" in association with "evil" further explained the meaning of evil, or did it just give us something to focus on that furthered somebody's agenda in this situation? There is no mention of the etymology of the word or its origin, which happens to be France. Below is the Wikipedia version found on the internet under "define terrorist - etymology", at http://en.wikipedia.org/wiki/Terrorist.

Main article: **Definition of terrorism**

"The term "terrorism" comes from the French word terrorisme, which is based on the Latin language verbs terrere (to frighten) and deterrere (to frighten from). It dates to 1795 when it was used to describe the actions of the Jacobin Club in their rule of Revolutionary France, during the so-called "Reign of Terror." Jacobins are rumored to have coined the term "terrorists" to refer to themselves. Acts described as Jacobin Club "terrorisme" were mostly cases of arrest and execution of opponents as a means of frightening the "enemies of the Revolution."

The United Nations Office for Drug Control and Crime Prevention has proposed a short legal definition —that "[an act of terrorism is] the peacetime equivalent of a war crime." A US court found that "the malice associated with terrorist attacks transcends even that of premeditated murder." Flatow v. Iran: Order. CA No. 97-396 (RCL)"

Both the Webster and the Wikipedia version have more broad and inclusive points of view about this subject area, but Encarta seems quite comfortable making the choice of delivering somewhat biased information as if it is neutral. In fact it seems to use this methodology often when defining what it seems to consider subjective definitions which define manner of thinking or seeing the world, and yet does not do the same thing when defining seemingly less flexible definitions

What does all this mean in the spiritual sense? Somebody or bodies at Encarta opened door number one, and bypassed doors number two and three. They did not challenge themselves and their beliefs in order to deliver the most neutral explanation of "evil", and then built further on their lack of neutrality with the supporting definitions. Why? Was it so much more work to try and give a neutral point of view considering the weight a dictionary has, or did someone, or some people make the choice to stop at their own limited thinking and agenda? Part of why we are going to hell in a hand basket as a world, is because we have become spiritually lazy and arrogant. From a spiritual standpoint, they might have taken what looks like the easiest door. Each action, that each of us takes, affects so many more than just ourselves. Think of all the young minds that have been influenced by this limited and loaded point of view.

There is one more thing about this kind of slant toward uneven actions. God looks for us to correct ourselves and choose the right door. What is happening lately, is that too many of us, too often, choose door number one and so the world is all out of whack and destroying itself. We have been mislead by some religions to believe that magically, God will save us and we will all be alright no matter what kind of mess we create here with our bad decisions. Think again. I have it from the horse's mouth so to speak. It ain't necessarily so . . .

CHAPTER FOURTEEN

HOW DOES GOD SEE US AND OUR LITTLE CLASSROOM?

I will try and convey this concept as closely as possible to how it has been explained to me.

We are all spirits on a fairly long journey. As spirits, we can never die, only the bodies that encapsulate us can die. If we like the bodies, we can learn and work to find ways to make it last, but by the nature of this classroom – Earth – we can try as we may, but still the body will fall by the wayside. Our earthly bodies are not God's real concern, only what we've learned while we are in this particular state. Therefore, begging to preserve the body if the spirit is not advancing is not useful.

We are not allowed to regress much (makes you wonder what Hitler was before), so if we show signs of unstoppable, unfaltering regression, we are called home, released from our bodies and go back to a neutral state to reevaluate and ascertain where we went wrong. At that point we are tasked with how to improve our learning experience, before we return to this planet or another for further training. If we experience pain and suffering during one lifetime, generally this means we either caused it in this lifetime, a prior lifetime, and/or there is something to be learned from this pained experiencing.

We generally have five exit points which are pre-arranged places in our lives, during which we are likely to return home if we are not progressing or if we have learned all the lessons we were due to learn that lifetime. From that state, we return home for evaluation and preparation for new lessons. This is generally true. However God is God, and can do whatever She chooses, so if He sees that we might have an opportunity to progress past what was expected, even though we may not have used any exit points, or if we have used all of them, She may decide to start us on a new lesson plan without bringing us home first if it appears we can handle it. This scenario is tantamount to skipping a class with the teacher's permission.

In my case, I had certain lessons to learn, in which the beginning of an awareness of clairvoyance and clairaudience were developing. But when I encountered another spirit who was sort of in the same boat of ending his life's lessons and having an opportunity to start anew, I was catapulted into another learning phase without having to leave here. It was my relationship with this other spirit, my twin flame, and the introduction of the malevolent spirit named Parker Drake who I mentioned earlier and who was attempting to make his life quite miserable, that prompted my changeover to another lifetime of lessons. Apparently I learned all that I was expected to in this lifetime rapidly, and was still moving forward and had only passed one exit point, so I was allowed to transition to another set of lessons without having to leave first. However it was not an easy transition and I questioned my sanity daily for about 11 months.

In another instance, I know a man who has used four of his exit points. He has recently exhibited such massive progress that his time may be extended so he can reach his goals in this lifetime—even if this means missing his fifth exit point. He was in danger of not doing so before, but is picking up his growth spurt, so I've been told. Recently, I had a client who was given 18 exit points so that she could learn to feel the pull of death, but not actually move toward it, as she had been a suicide person for several lifetimes. Keeping her positive had not worked, but making her constantly trying to move toward it seems to be working better.

God does not particularly have any feeling about our death, except that it is the end of a training session, so begging about living and no pain, etc. means little to Her if there is no lesson to be learned. In the scheme of things, death is usually quite a short process, unless its length is also to teach something. Pain however, can sometimes be avoided if it doesn't interfere with the lesson, or if it enhances the lesson or lessons for the spirits experiencing it.

For instance, I prayed very hard for several months that my father not experience pain from the effects of cancer after he found out he was no longer in remission, and there was no remaining treatment that he would take seriously. After several conversations with God, I was told finally that this would be granted for as long as possible, but that the last two weeks of his life would probably have pain because there was no choice given the lessons he was to learn, and the type of care he was undergoing, or more accurately, refusing. If we do not interfere with God's plans, asking for leniency is sometimes granted. Know that God is an interactive, hands-on God at all times, no matter what some religions teach or what seems logical from the state of the world.

Given my father's personality and incredible strong will and ego, this lack of pain in his terminal condition, convinced him that there was nothing wrong with him as we all had thought. In fact, he did not even believe he had cancer. Even when he wasted away from 160 to 116 pounds, and had been battling cancer for nearly twenty years, he did not believe in the diagnosis and thought his entire family was all crazy. This situation became so bizarre that my sisters began to believe he had gone into remission too, despite the fact that his bodily functions were ceasing, he was barely able to walk, but still there was no pain. It got somewhat ridiculous, and I asked God if I should not have interfered by asking, and should he return to an unencumbered state, though I still did not wish pain on him. I was in a direct spiritual quagmire about addressing and processing what is desired and what is needed. I talked to my most open-minded sister who agreed that prayer must work because she was seeing evidence to that effect, but no, having pain was not better than being out of touch with reality. All the doctors were amazed and pretty much in disbelief.

The last year of my father's life was a long, rough year. No one, including perhaps God, the doctors and me expected him to live beyond two months. God had said that my father's will as a spirit might override the exit point as he was still learning some things throughout the ordeal, and as I said, God can do anything. Still the results were unexpected. That is exactly what happened, and he lived long past physical expectations. He was only at his third exit point, so he could have gone on theoretically, had the flesh been willing. He had begun to learn important new lessons about love and tolerance that he clearly had not known before, and thus he was allowed to continue for a while.

God called him a fascinating spirit and testament to the will of spirit beings and said that it was all going just as it should: my asking, God's granting, and my father's reaction to the lack of pain. He lived almost a year past reason, physically speaking, and was only in pain during the last month and a half maybe of his life. Even then, it was not as severe as it should have been medically speaking, and he took only aspirin until the last few weeks when he moved to light morphine. He was walking with a walker and talking until he had a stroke during the last week before he died and finally resigned himself to leaving because he could not abide being out of control and misunderstood due to the resultant speech difficulties.

I learned an important lesson, which is why in part, I believe I was allowed to participate in what was primarily my father's lesson. God is all-powerful, which I knew, but am always awestruck when it is evidenced, and we have the power to do so much more than we utilize.

Another concept was cemented as well for me. Our purpose here is to learn. We are in essence recyclable, and to fool ourselves into thinking that God sees it any other way is fairly ludicrous, especially if we are waiting on Him to rescue us. It is averse to our learning directive and Her job as teacher for Her to save us. Saving ourselves comes through how quickly and easily we get the lessons and move on to the next. The body is immaterial, but the spirit is paramount. It is the spirit we are training.

The concept of evil is connected with exercise of human will. Most things that we perceive as evil, we create. With our will, mind and spirit, we can create all kinds of energy states, the likes of which you can't imagine and recognize that we have done to ourselves. Though I get vague answers about this when I broach the subject, since God only gives us the lessons we are truly ready for, there probably is no supreme dark spirit like Satan. However, we can create energy through our spiritual actions that we recognize as Satanic or all the other "evil" stuff we conjure up. It is very, very real energy, but I'm unsure now as to whether or not it comes from some evil central location, or that we conjure it up and God allows it for our education. We can create spiritual evil from our fears and spiritual bankruptcy that looks like demonic possession, and in that state, we can draw more negative energy to us that will heighten and exacerbate the situation so much that it can assume almost any form.

As I progress in my lessons and can process information ahead of time, rather than it just happening upon me as it did the first three years, my questions get more complex, but the answers get simpler. So when I ask about things like the existence of evil, clearly I am being forced to use new skills to evaluate my lessons. When that happens, I get my new standard answer for most of this year, which is "What do you think?" Hmmmm.

What I know is this: The higher your vibratory level, the less negative energy you create yourself, and the less negative energy can come around and stick. That's why prayer works in exorcisms. We align ourselves with God more closely during this ritual, as well as a person who presumably stays more aligned with God, a Priest, and all things come through Him. The purpose of demonic possession, stalking by errant spirits, etc., may well be to force our own spirits to reconnect to God and stay attached. I do know that negative spirits don't visit me anymore, knock on wood. They just don't come around. They find order somehow, and no level of acceptable chaos because of my connection to God and the manner in which I am growing. Thus, I'm not much fun to be around for them so they don't bother hanging around.

Yesterday, I was looking at the candles I have lit for the different Saints, Deities, Orisha in my house. Despite what some religions dictate, God does not discriminate, and evolved spirits do not compete with each other for human spirits' attention and affection,. Therefore, they are all responsive to any human spirit who is working hard and asking for guidance. That is not to say that they don't have rules and preferences, but it is not nearly as rigid as many religions teach. I was walking through a room that has five continuously lit (since the late 1990's) candles in it, and I noticed that I was able to see the light from the candles beam up to the ceiling of the room. I could always see the candle's flame the way that most people do with a sort of energy haze and waving glow for about three or four inches above the candle, but this was different. This viewing was clearly a shift in my energy reading ability.

Curious, I looked at the candles, and realized that I could see this elongated energy beam in all of them. As the day went on (considering that I started watching them in the pre-dawn dark because I get up very early), I realized that I could still see the beams during the daylight. They were in proportion to the flame, but went straight up like a transporter beam from Star Trek – a true "beam me up Scotty" shaft of light. God pays attention to our denial systems, and usually will make things quite clear for us when a statement manifested through physical awareness is being made.

In other words, if we concentrate on raising our vibrations, rather than lowering them, we will create and attract positive energy, rather then creating and attracting negative energy. With that simple understanding, we have the basis for things like demonic possession and healing with energy like the "laying of hands" folks, Pranic Healers, or Mahi Kari practitioners. If we understand how we are designed to connect to God, then we get closer to understanding how God sees us, and how She expects us to function and thereby will interact with us. It's actions toward us then become demystified, and the course of action and plan for growth become much easier to identify and determine.

If we accept the concept that God is incredible energy (and this is supported by religions of almost every kind as well as science fiction, mathematics and science), then clearly, if we are trying to be the next God of a new universe and to build and possess all those traits, then it makes sense that we learn to see, manipulate and deal with energy in new and different ways. The increased awareness and utilization of that energy for the highest good, ours and the world's, is our individual primary directive and goal. Therefore, when we get closer to understanding this concept and moving in that direction, which first requires letting go of fears on a daily basis, and making strong attempts to connect directly with and through God, then we are meeting our goal to move closer to God and Godlike behavior and we are supported by Her in this endeavor.

God sees us as "gods in progress", though She knows that many will fall short because many of us didn't figure things out or chose to stop at a level before reaching that point even when they know it to be possible. He starts us at our most basic level as spirits, and puts challenges and obstacles in front of us that will encourage or require us to grow and seek to become the most even-handed, gentlest, kindest, fair-minded, unselfish, strong, powerful, efficient, fluid, quick moving, unstuck, flexible, tolerant beings that we can be. He waits for us to comprehend each lesson, and he graduates us when we have progressed through each phase. He does not punish us for our shortcomings, but will allow us to create our own difficulties when we lose sight of the primary objective and get caught up in our own fears, greed, narrow mindedness, etc.,. In part, when we have disasters happen, it is not punishment as some religious folks would see it, but an opportunity for the rest of us to change and become our best spiritual selves. These so called large scale catastrophes are opportunities for us to rise to our best spiritual training and activity level and become our best selves.

Since the spirit never dies, and that is God's primary concern, incomprehensible as it may seem to some, it means nothing to allow a planet to wipe itself out with greed (wars), disease (AIDS for example), selfishness (natural disasters, God's occasional response to our lack of concern for one another) and all other manner of horrors we create, so that the remaining spirits can utilize the opportunities to raise their spiritual awareness, connectivity and general vibrational level. The bodies that are lost are only spirits who travel home to reassess for the next class session. The more we learn, the more we understand how to connect to God, and thereby the greater progress the spirit is able to make. That is Her goal for us. The rest constitutes fabrications we conjure for ourselves so that we can feel comfortable.

What this means is that material happenings are seldom in correlation with spiritual lessons. God's lessons are not really rewards or punishments, although it appears that they are sometimes used as collective training sessions for those affected and for those remaining. For instance, a hurricane that wipes out thousands may have been allowed to do so to encourage more souls who remain to get on the right track again, and to bring out a collective goodness in the rest of us. Remember, physical death means nothing to God, nothing. Cold as it may sound, the people who died probably have an array of lessons that a death in that manner will heighten for their spiritual growth. Those who don't need that same lesson probably left beforehand, or couldn't get a flight back. However, it is not punishment, but the activity needed to further each spirit's growth. They just happened to be in the same place, but make no mistake, that was part of God's plan too. Our lives are an intricate series of events put into motion by a master teacher. Each person is individually placed in each position and/or situation to afford us the opportunity for maximum spiritual growth. Although we may have collective situations for our growth, we are still growing individually for our ultimate goal, to be the next God.

Generally speaking however, no two individuals experience life's lesson in the same manner. To say we have cookie cutter lessons and a "standard" treatment of a situation, like "just work hard and you will be successful" is totally inaccurate. It all depends upon the lesson. Otherwise, we would all be able to play ball like Michael Jordan or Joe Namath, or we would all be rich like the Rockefellers, or look like Raquel Welch, George Clooney or Halle Berry. This misconception makes for a world of nonsense. We do not all come here with the same equipment because we do not all have the same lessons. Therefore sayings like "work hard and you will always succeed", or "the law of attraction will always rule", or "you reap what you sow" just aren't necessarily true, and it is shortsighted and a gross oversimplification for us to think so. To some degree, belief in such adages is childish, and we have so much evidence to the contrary that I'm amazed at how people can hold on to such notions. That is not to say that they don't have their place, but it is not a simple place. The types of life experiences we have all depends upon the lesson we were sent to learn. Though we might be reaping what we sow, it might not have anything to do with what we sow in this lifetime. We need a more sophisticated, spiritual in tune view of the spiritual world.

Using my life as an example, I have a very difficult, though not impossible life, materially speaking. I am by no means under the kind of hardships that homeless people and starving Africans are enduring, but none-the-less, it is not easy. I do contract work, and no matter how hard I work, only one in 30 ventures actually results in money. So I am always near foreclosure and never financially secure. This may well be in part because I must have this experience in order to explain it to you in this book. My primary lesson at this moment in this lifetime is endurance. I have people all around me who put in minimum effort and have maximum results. I put in incredible effort and have few things actually succeed, however materially speaking, I never go completely under, but am often on the edge of material disaster. Yes, I can speak with God, and it does me a world of good spiritually speaking, but virtually no good materially speaking. I am writing this book, with the full understanding that it may only be bought by 10 people, but I am confident that they are the 10 God's wants to have this information. Surprised?

If you are surprised that's because we live in a world of "money for faith" mentality. The monetary prosperity index we hear about on television for religion is high, but I assure you, it has nothing to do with God. It's a sales mechanism, because few would buy into a system in which the truth is told. Furthermore, how would all those mega preachers be able to buy new Rolls Royces? The truth is that your particular lesson plan runs your show, and whatever God determines makes you clear and focused within that lesson, is what will happen.

I am a catalyst for other people's growth, and my personal lesson at this time is endurance, consistency and fortitude. When other people need work, I can find it for them in a hurry – usually within hours, as well as having access to hoards of other material opportunities that I have been able to provide people. But for my personal financial existence, I barely get by. This has been the case for nearly two decades, despite the fact that I put in on average 12 hours of work per day, usually 6 days per week, and am respected in my field. Doesn't make sense?

If this doesn't make sense, it may be because we have been trained that God rewards His believers. She does, but not generally materially as so many ministers today would have you believe. If that happens, it is either part of God's plan in order to help us grow in this life, or a future one. All things are about our growth and building spiritual strength.

Below is my personal reading/message from the end of December, 2005, during the writing of this book. Remember, I have not said that I was any wiser than any other person, only that I can hear. I also struggle with my own attitudes despite my understanding of the big picture. I am human and faulty. Anyone who is operating at a really high level, you won't see on this plane. They don't have to come back here. I'm a telephone line, and in being so, I might make just slightly faster progress than many because I can get the messages more often. Even in my dumbest state, I ought to be able to find new ways to operate, but the more I find, the harder the lessons, like one might imagine a nearly endless school to be.

This was my reading. Remember, God has a sense of humor and can speak to us in the manner we find most comfortable, therefore the language She uses with me is fairly familiar. However, It can get quite formal when He wants to make a more emphatic point, or if I border on disobedience. We will talk about that as well. It's no fun! Another point that might make this clearer is the fact that I am painfully shy and slow to approach unproven and unfamiliar entities without a lot of trepidation. This is also what the voice of God sounds like each morning when I pray and ask for guidance. Sometimes, as after this listening/reading, I might wait a day before I want to talk again.

"12-28-05

God: You must work on a continuous basis. You must not be afraid of contact with anyone because of any reason. You must be more fearless in your business dealings and not wait for anyone to do it for you. You are capable of everything, so everything that you do not feel you can do, you must learn. You must make yourself better qualified in all things for the sake of it, and you must stay in that mode at all times. You must not ask why things don't happen, but you must go make them happen. Yours will not ever be an easy road, and so you cannot act as if it will ever compare to anyone else you know. You can work 9 times harder and still not get the same result as others around you, and that will always be. You are not to whine about it, and no you are not allowed to leave this situation to go somewhere peaceful and quiet to study and learn to rise and levitate. That is not going to be your task in this life. Yours is to work a lot with lots of disappointments and very little material gain, and almost no moral satisfaction because that is what you came here to learn, massive endurance. That is the way it will be. The only way that can change to some extent, materially speaking is if others care for you. This has all been said to you, and it is no different now. It just seems different because you are tired. It will not likely end in this lifetime.

Eva: So trying to get this present project done is useless?

God: Not at all, it just won't be easy, or even moderately difficult. It will be unbearably difficult, as will all things in your life. However if you survive this life in that way, with all these difficulties and remain to be your best self, you will be amazed at what will happen spiritually speaking. That is your goal. To have dreams, skill, but unless you are working very hard, none of it will happen, but even if you do, only part of it will come to fruition, and you must bear it and be calm with that as a reality. The more you endure, the more will be put upon you to endure, and the more you do that with ease and acceptance, the better your spiritual progress.

Eva: So it is my attitude that causes this to be more difficult?

God: No, it will be difficult. Your attitude causes you to hurt more because of it. That is all that is happening, but it won't help so why do it. You will always struggle, and you will always have difficult relationships and that is the way that it will be.

Eva: How might I alter this?

God: To some extent, you cannot. But the best thing to do is work harder and with resignation so that it is easier to endure.

Eva: I find it hard to believe that you would put someone here to just have hell their whole lives, and that is the point of it.

God: Believe it. Endurance is your task, incredible endurance. Nothing else really matters. Whereas one in 3 things that they attempt to accomplish will be the result for most of the people around you, your ratio will be one in 35. And even then it will not go easily, and it may only succeed in a half state, requiring you to do more work to get it complete. That is your life.

Eva: Why would you relegate anyone to this? Is it punishment?

God: No. It builds endurance and stamina and you need them for the manner in which you are developing. Stop whining about it and questioning it. Just accept it and you will fare better. That is the way it is.

Eva: How might I best survive this?

God: Work, and make the 35 times come closer together so that you can build more resistance to the negative times in between. In other words, it is taking you 3 to 4 months to reach your 35 times now, and it is because of that that you are having these huge ebb and flows. Put more work into a shorter amount of time and then it will be less disastrous, less often seemingly. That will stabilize you a bit more.

Eva: I'm not sure I believe this at all.

God: Then don't, and it is assured that you will stay in this same position. Work harder and more consistently and the odds will seem less and less damaging.

Eva: I reject this.

God: If you'd like. We'll see how that goes."

Well that's enough to make you jump out of bed each morning and say "Man it's good to be alive!" right? Actually though, it really is, because I am no longer in the dark. For years, I suspected this, but it made no sense because I also believed in the power of positive thinking as a self determining tool, and that if you work hard and do what is right, you will reap God's rewards. I now know this is a naïve interpretation of a complex spiritual world, and certainly does not apply in any material sense and one has nothing to do with the other.

The above were a group of questions asked in great frustration over something that seemed to be happening within a week, has now taken five months, and has proved massively complicated when the resolution should have been easy. I keep hoping that I have passed some mark and this situation will be lessened, but that shows a lack of spiritual maturity on my part. I am almost through it, and I hope I will not ask what I already know again out of frustration. I am nearly resigned, but when it gets particularly difficult, I will at least ask. I no longer attempt boxing matches with God. I learned firsthand that my arms are way too short.

The reason I said that I rejected this, was because God does not always tell you the truth, and though all evidence points to it being true given my history, there is always a difficult balance between what God tells us and where God leads us. They don't always look just alike, and might conflict. There I said it, and for those who are clinging onto the simplified explanations of some religions, this is a hard concept to swallow, but it is true. God will do whatever it takes to walk us through our journey to higher spiritual awareness. If what we consider to be a lie is appropriate and will do the trick then He will lie to us, and that is all there is to it. It is unwise to think that we know enough to know how God ought to do Her job. We do not and unless we get very close to being the "One" as the Matrix called it, we are not likely to, even when we can hear and are told. That brings us to the nature of God.

CHAPTER FIFTEEN
THE NATURE OF GOD

This is perhaps the most fascinating of all the subjects in this book. Possibly because what I now know is counter to almost everything I was taught, and yet, if you look at the nature of the Bible – particularly the old testament – there are glimpses of truth, and a whole lot of wishful thinking and interpretation. The easiest way to explain it is that God is not simple, is chameleon like, changeable according to how well we get the lesson, and can whip around and do the most unexpected things imaginable. Additionally, She will not tell you to do anything wrong, unless He thinks that you have the lesson down and shouldn't be stupid enough to do it. If you do begin to act upon whatever suggestion She might have made that was wrong that was designed as a test, if you are in prayer It will not allow you to actually execute the wrong. But the chastisement for being spiritually questionable is not at all worth your not thinking through the task in the first place, and you are not likely to do anything as stupid again. This is all clear if you are paying attention. If not, it all just looks like chaos and confusion, and that God is not paying attention.

If you were raised, like I was, to believe that God is some sort of monolithic stoic creature reaching down from the heavens to touch us, and you hold onto that, then you might find what I am about to say uncomfortable. The best way to explain this is to give you a few examples.

THE NEW DISCOVERY

A couple of days after my "porch" incident I began to feel a little more confident that God was actually speaking to me. At that point, it dawned upon me, neophyte fool that I was, that all my problems would then be over because all I had to do was ask God to guide me every step of the way, in all actions, at all times. Sounds like a nice little prayer when you say it in church, and though you don't know you have a direct connection to God because He is still up in the sky reaching down to touch your little hand, that is where He is – detached. It is a whole different enchilada when you can hear every word She says. So you say this little naïve prayer born of part fact, part fairytale mythology and think you have solved everything and now have the answer to life. You think you will have it made just doing what you are told.

God will agree, as She did in my case, and say okay, if that is what you want. Then He proceeded to tell me everything. The next hour went something like this while I was cooking dinner:

"Okay, now walk over to the refrigerator and open the door. Reach in and get the lettuce, tomatoes, carrots and red cabbage. Good, now close the door and walk back to the island and take the sharpest knife out of the holder . . . no, not that one, that one is not sharp enough, use the one with the knobbed handle, yes, that one, and now wash the cabbage first, and begin cutting it up. That's good, but the pieces are too large. Make the cuts narrower, no that's too wide, make them more slender. Now scrape the outer layer of the carrots, and wash them. That's right, use the scrub brush over the sink, not the one in the drawer . . ."

Because it was God, and I'd been taught like most of us not to defy God, I tried my best to deal with this. I made it about an hour before I finally said that I didn't want quite that much input. Then She asked if that was not what I had requested? I, of course, replied that it was not quite in the form I wanted. So, being God, and the way He operates said, well what did you mean? That of course meant that I then had to figure it out. She listened carefully before telling me that it was good that I was beginning to realize that it was not Its job to live my life. I wasn't allowed to turn that over in any form, not even to Him, because it was my job, my purpose in this life, to learn as much as possible, process the information and move toward maximum growth.

The first thing to recognize is that God has a flair for the dramatic.

THE TEST

When it became clear that I really was talking to God, I began to ask, 'Why me?' and what purpose this had in life because surely it was bigger than the direction I was headed. I tried to figure out what I was supposed to do, and somehow, the school of religion came into my focus, first suggested by an ancestor from four generations before, and then solidified as a concept by God. I decided to prepare to apply for graduate school. I am dyslexic, and this condition shows up in mathematics more than in written form. I have always been terrible in any and all forms of math and never took any courses past Algebra. Even then, I made horrible grades and never understood it. So when I was preparing for the Graduate Review Exam, I just couldn't understand the math section of the test preparation materials and never did better than a 300 on any of the several practice exams. I was in my mid forties and just not getting it, as I never had before either. So after an honest, frustrating effort to master the math section, and many attempts to see if my guess ratio might get me a score high enough to make a decent grade, which it didn't, I asked God what was supposed to happen in this case. She said, do your best and have faith that it will work out, and that I didn't have to understand higher math concepts for where I was going (that should have been a red flag). So I did. I prepared for the verbal section and went in to take the test.

People talk about miracles as if they are something special to God. They are only special to us because they are usually so far beyond our comprehension. That is because we are miniscule, and God is all-powerful. We tend to forget that and think that somehow we are in the same arena. How absurd. It is a concept that we think we understand, but most of the time we do not truly operate under full comprehension of how vast the difference is. In a way, miracles are reminders for us of the expansion between our abilities and God's. For God they are just part of the job, like "time to make the doughnuts!" As I write this, I realize that as usual, God is right. My voice and its matter of fact approach, is probably appropriate to help demystify our relationship with God. Though some will find this blasphemous, they probably won't continue to read. This book is for those folks who believe that what is popular and pervasive isn't always enough or accurate.

So I went to take the GRE, wondering how foolish I would likely look when I got to the math section. The day before I took the test was the last time I had contact with God, and Her words were "Have faith." I tried to speak to Her while driving to the test location, but got no answer. It is these moments when you question your sanity in the beginning, and lean toward feeling real foolishness. It is also these moments when you simply must do what you are told and have faith.

I sat down to take the test, asking if God was there as I began. I wondered if I might have been set up for something when again I got no answer. I questioned whether or not humiliation had to be part of my life's lesson, and hadn't I learned enough humiliation already? Still there was no answer. Fear of being so identifiably stupid almost made me run out of the door, but I didn't because on the other side of that was memory of a voice I could no longer hear saying "have faith." So I did. I took a deep breath and started the test.

I got through the verbal and asked once if She was there because I sure could have used some help on a couple of those questions. The qualitative writing test came up, and I wrote the two answers. Then it was time for the math. I clicked on the screen to begin the math section and heard Her voice in a male form and formal tone, which by then was not usually used with me.

"Hello, I am here." He said quite calmly, "Listen to what I am saying carefully. Do not try to help. Read every question in your mind, exactly as it is written, with the letter choices before each answer and I will give you the answer to each question. You don't need to try and help. Do you understand?"

I said yes, and once again was grateful that I wasn't insane, at least not completely. So we began. Now a really absurd thing happens on this journey, even with so much evidence and information. Because as I said, we don't grasp what miracles really are, we think it has something to do with us somehow. Sounds crazy I know, but after the first few questions, I began to try and help! I felt guilty somehow for getting so much help and not actually doing the test myself. I was in minor turmoil because 1), it was happening – God was giving me the answers; 2) I was not pulling my own weight and I had been taught to do so my entire life; 3) I can only chalk up to utter stupidity! But guess what? I'm pretty sure that God knew that also, hence that phrase "don't try and help." The good thing for me was that I couldn't be much help. After a couple of instances of me saying "Oh I think I can figure this one out", and then of course losing my mind trying to do so and probably, no definitely making a mess of the answer, I surrendered. God was quiet during my moments of insanity, and after I had frustrated myself the second time, I asked "Why am I doing this?" And He said, "I have no idea. Maybe you ought to figure that out. Do you want to take this time to do so, or would you like to continue with the test?"

Well duh . . . not only does God have a flair for the dramatic, but She is a comedienne as well. I opted to finish the test and so we proceeded, with me reading and Him giving me the answers. At some point I said during this growth session, "you know if I get too high of a score along the way, somebody might actually think I know some math." He said, "I've taken that into account." So we finished the test. I read the questions, He gave me the answers.

Now it would be easy enough to once again decide I was crazy and making most of this up-- no matter how clearly those little people in my head spoke. At the end of the test the computer allowed you to see your test score on the math and verbal sections. The qualitative writing scores had to be evaluated later. My math score was 450, and certainly not of my own accord! I gathered up the one scratch sheet from the few questions I had attempted and got myself out of there. I asked God later if I had correctly answered the questions I'd attempted. She said no.

When I got my score for the qualitative/writing portion, it was a 6.0, the highest score possible. I applied to a couple of good schools that had programs that I thought I would like and was rejected. I am not a school person. Love to learn and hate school. So I began to question what this exercise was really about. I asked if I should continue to pursue school, and was asked if I wanted to -- another trick question. I said that I didn't know I had a choice, and that I thought I had been told to do this. I was asked if I could remember the actual conversation in which She told me I had to go to school, and of course I couldn't, which is why I write down all conversations now. It had sort of come in suggestions for a direction mostly from my great, great, great grandmother when I really tried to put it together again. God's input was really more like, "that sounds like a good idea." I'd been set up, but what for? It would take a while for all the pieces to come together.

Over the next couple of months, I began to understand. I do a lot of writing and had ventured out to write some fiction. I won't go into too many details, but let it suffice to say that my style, as you might have noticed, is not for everyone. I have a friend who is perhaps the most difficult personality I have ever seen and certainly ever known.

She is good as gold in so many ways and will not abandon you when you are in need if she is in agreement with the nature of that need, and can understand it. In these circumstances she can be gentle and supportive as you could ever know. By the same token, she is mean to the core in other ways and very, very catty, delivering comments that are meant to cut deep and destroy. She would never recognize herself like this, but I do now recognize her to be like this sometimes. Overcoming this flaw is clearly her task to conquer in this lifetime. In one reading, God referred to her as "the rock against which all of the rest of you will break."

For the couple of years before taking the GRE, she fed me almost daily doses of doubt about my writing. First she said she couldn't read the book I had written because it had so many problems. She also claimed that potential readers wouldn't really think like the book, and I was too unusual, odd and unclear in my thinking. Before I made the book available to the public, she made sure I knew of another friend who had written a children's book was doing "real" work because she was self-publishing the book and living her craft – which by omission, of course I was not. By the time I took the GRE and made a perfect score on the writing portion, I had listened to her telling me what a failure I was as a writer for at least six or seven years. Daily, there was some reference about why I was obviously inadequate as a writer since nobody was really buying my work. Still, I know that as much as she is able, she loves me. She just has many more lessons to learn about the nature of love, as I have about boundaries. She doesn't know how to love freely. I believe this is a product of subtle parental emotional abuse and clearly something she came to work through on the spiritual side. Remember, God is a chemist, so we did not come together by accident. We are designed to learn from other members of our Study Group.

One day, confused about the reason I had taken the test, and losing interest in religion as a subject to study formally, I asked what could possibly be the reason for going through all those essays, applications, preparing for and taking the GRE. God asked what I had learned. My answer, which came without hesitation, was the score of the test proved I was a good solid writer which was tremendously comforting to know. Now this is somewhat ridiculous because I had made whatever living to this point in my life on my ability to write, but my friend's daily dose of doubt filling comments always made me question my abilities. Coupled with the fact that I never make enough money from my writing, and for other spiritual reasons I had not pieced together at that time, it was hard to work around the obstacles. God asked, "Do you trust the opinion of the test evaluators?" And I said yes. She answered, "Then if you know that, no one can ever make you doubt that you are a good writer again, can they? So maybe you won't allow it anymore."

There it was: The lesson. Elaborate, a lot of going around the barn, but still, it was clear. So what was this year long exercise about?

1. I needed to know for myself that I had strong ability in a skill I needed, loved and used everyday, no matter who tried to make me doubt myself at the core.
2. I needed to recognize what my friend had been doing, intentionally or because of her own damaged life, because it stopped completely the moment I realized that I needed to make sure nobody could make me doubt this ability unless I gave them permission and participated.
3. It also made me know how much spiritual ground she had to cover that I had not recognized previously, though she had been giving me headaches for years. Still I thought the problem was personality differences. It was not. It is spiritual differences and effort to progress. She fights hard to stay the same. I fight hard to learn.
4. It made me understand the true nature of a gray spirit (which she is).
5. It helped me to understand the nature of God better and how, when the lesson is important, She will see us through to the graduation as long as we trust and have faith.
6. It better defined the nature of my relationship to formal religion, as I felt inadequate without more training. Through further discussions about school, I learned that it was my own self-doubt, and not God's that made me jump on the need to learn more and be adequate when it was only mildly suggested as a possibility. When you get right down to it, the notion is foolish. I have the most qualified teacher

possible, bar none, so how absurd to think that people guessing and postulating about the nature of God could tell me more than God Himself!

7. It gave me a better understanding of the creativity and complexities of our lessons and how they rarely turn out to be what they look like. And more importantly, how seldom God will clue you in before you get to the end of that section.

Of course, as usual, God was right. I never allowed my friend to question my abilities again without a clear response from me. After stopping her gently once by pointing out that the test scorers were better judges of my writing than she was, she never tried again. She has looked for my other weak spots though, as that is her way, till she chooses to do it differently. I have no idea what she thinks she is accomplishing, but I fear a repeat life is in store for her to work this out if she doesn't accomplish more in this present life.

THE SIDE STEP

I know a man who has a nightmare for a wife. She is selfish, childish, mean, controlling, and generally not a person you want to be near. For some reason this marriage worked for him in the early years, but it is not working so well after a decade. She has run off almost every one of his friends along with some clients, and has made his work and life beyond difficult. She complains that he does not bring in enough money and works daily to undermine his self-esteem. Now that I know him better I understand that he allows this abuse by spiritual invitation. He is resolving his own serious character issues, and he has received her as a lesson.

There are children involved, and rather than leave, he seemed trapped in this relationship for years. He experienced the following incident that seemed to prompt some growth. The wife managed to destroy his good work situation because she wanted him to get a more traditional, full time job. He found a job in lieu of continuing freelancing, which he liked more and did well in before she worked to alienate his income flow.

I asked God if this new position was going to work. Clearly the problem was not the job, it was allowing this mad woman to run his life into the ground and standing by and watching it as if he was helpless. God said, "Of course not." I just figured the wife would do her normal thing and alienate her husband's new boss. But never forget that God is the Creator of all things, and He is sometimes quite creative! It also never pays to second guess God.

My friend started work on Monday, called Tuesday to say that he liked the job, though he thought it would take some getting used to, but he saw no problems. On Wednesday he threw his back out so badly he could not move and called me for the name of my chiropractor. His injury was bad, and on Friday, he was fired.

After I saw him and made sure he was basically alright, I couldn't stop laughing. This type of reaction seems to be a negative side effect of this hearing thing. When you see how absurd people are, including myself, when we try and sidestep lessons instead of meeting things head on, it truly does get comical. People don't tend to share my levity in these situations. I do find the gyrations we go through hilarious-- thinking we run something and trying to maneuver around apparent paths that God has put in front of us. My friend didn't really appreciate my laughter, but he is fairly good-natured when he is stable, and just stared at me like I was nuts.

When you think you can get around the lesson, God will let you know quickly who really runs this show. We should never forget that this is school, and if you are failing a class, there will be repercussions designed to get you back on track. It was shortly after this incident, after years of not really paying attention to what was going on because recognition might require change, that my friend seems to have finally taken a long hard look at his role in his dysfunctional marriage. I asked him one day about two months or so before he was hurt, if he thought that his wife was crazy and he was the sane one between the two of them. He said, after some thought, "Yeah, I suppose that is accurate." At the time, he generally spoke honestly, which was one of his most admirable traits. I responded that in my opinion (which I recognized he had not asked for), he was way crazier then she was because his behavior allowed her crazy behavior thereby encouraging it. He looked at me like I had two heads.

In summary, God has an incredible sense of humor. He is interactive and thoroughly engaged in our lives. It has infinite patience, and can be very creative when we are stubborn and hardheaded, and refuse to get the lessons usually plainly placed before us. Most of all, when doing Her job, She can be relentless in the pursuit of our growth. Our job is to grow.

CHAPTER SIXTEEN
RESISTANCE EQUALS RETARDATION

I believe that there should be something called the "theory of forced non-growth." I call it that because when we are not in opposition, our natural state is to grow. If we allowed things to flow naturally and move at the rate that they ideally should, and always chose door number two or three, more often than not we would move at an appropriate pacc and stay spiritually mobile. But when we try and force things to do what we want, bending and yielding to our commands usually in order to keep things comfortable, we are often in direct conflict with the natural order of life and therefore with the order that God designed for us in this life's lesson plan. Thus we become stagnant and retard our own spiritual growth.

Sometimes it is difficult to tell what our natural order actually is because we live in a society that is highly individualistic. It is very easy to fool ourselves into believing that we are the captain of our ship, and should be allowed to do whatever and all that we choose. If that overrides the obvious -- which is that we are one of many and captain of nothing in the scheme of things, and certainly not in comparison to the awesome power of God -- then we could spend a lot of time trying to make a life fit into a self involved mold that wasn't appropriate in the first place. The more we try and make things fit our desires and self imposed mold, the more likely we are to choose the most appealing door (at least at first glance) number one, and the further and further out of focus the lesson gets.

This resistance to growth, this forced system of non-growth, will eventually slow our progress to a halt and make it necessary to get little reminders from the schoolmaster, God. Additionally, in the long run the system of non-growth only makes our lives much harder. Let's say for example that you are in the same job for 12 years, which you began disliking in about the 5th year, but you have kids, and a wife and blah, blah, blah. Part of the reason you hate the job is it requires so much time away from your family often on nights and weekends, but the pay is good.

Somewhere in that next year or so (between year 5 and 6 ½) you make a conscious or unconscious decision that to stay in that position is easier than leaving, thereby forcing yourself into non-growth. By doing so you've slowed whatever progress you should have made because you chose door number one. However, God doesn't usually let us stay in a non-growth mode without some pressure. So during the seventh year of working at this position, your son starts having problems with his fifth grade math. Your wife hated math in school and can't provide assistance to your son in this area. Your decision to keep this job directly impacts your son's situation. Instead of taking a job that might afford more time with him, you continue the job you hate and find a tutor. This is where the process of non-growth takes greater form and unnecessary complication with every decision and every misstep.

The job you currently have only makes ten thousand more a year than one that you can find that has the same benefits, the same tasks for the most part, but not the prestige, and not the perks--but more time for family bonding opportunities. Most importantly, you can be home by 6:00 to 6:30 every night, instead of 9:00 every night and working most Saturdays and some Sundays. So you decide, with your wife's agreement, that you should get your son a tutor at $150.00 per week, two days a week, for 50 weeks a year equaling $7,500.00 per year. You also have to provide money for public transportation for one of those weekly visits because your wife can only pick him up one day a week, which adds five dollars a week, equaling $250.00 per year. Your wife's gas to pick him up on the other day of tutoring is another $250.00. Now the total for your son's tutoring is $8,000.00, but this situation still deprives him of the parental attention that he could only get from you if you'd made helping your son a priority. Clearly, you have chosen door number one, the seemingly easy one, and believe me, God is paying attention to the choice.

For an extra $2,000.00 per year, you have missed your wife, and children's activities most evenings and weekends; and you have missed the connection and memories possible and available in the intimate action of teaching your child. Was it worth it?

The following year, your daughter has trouble with Spanish. Though you speak a little Spanish, you don't have time to spend with her. You locate a tutor, a neighbor college kid who is not a professional but a native speaker who is working for extra money for school. Her tutoring session, end up costing about $3,000.00 for the year. Your son has now moved into more advanced math, which you know how to do, but still can't do because of the hours at the job you hate. Now you are paying $11,000.00 in tutors, and you have to work a little harder to make up the difference in bonuses, etc., because now you are $1,000.00 in the hole.

Does this scenario now look like door number one, two or three? If you are standing on the outside, the choices don't look all that complicated. Yet, people on the inside who are not connecting to God and asking for guidance and then listening for answers that they don't create in their heads, will keep on moving toward what looks easiest. If at this point, considering God put this lesson in front of you, you still choose to stay at that job and find more money within those confines, you must ask yourself why. If you are staying for prestige, self-esteem, vanity, or any reason other than the spiritual growth you and your family will get from this experience, you are choosing door number one, which is usually the most self-involved door of them all.

You have to ask yourself in each of these cases, who gains and who loses, and to what degree? If your focus is on helping your loved one and yourself spiritually rather than materially, you are probably choosing door number three. If you are doing more for others spiritually, and you are not sure about yourself, you are probably choosing door number two and you might figure out what you gain spiritually later. If you are choosing the route that does more for yourself materially and egotistically than spiritually, that's door number one. Herein lies the challenge: to figure out how to judge these decisions reasonably so you can know which one to chose if you are trying hard to meet the challenges God has put before you. The only way to start this type of evaluation is to connect to the teacher and ask for guidance and then shut up long enough to hear the answer. If you try any other route, you are likely to miss the boat because as I said, this is an energy issue. We must be seeking to raise our vibrations so that we are closer to God and God's behavior and plan for us.

When we choose not to utilize this kind of system of evaluation for our decisions, we willingly and happily choose a mechanism of forced non-growth. If we do so repeatedly, we throw ourselves into resistance to what is being placed before us, and then voluntary spiritual retardation. The thing about this decision process is that if we don't master this system of determining our best method for spiritual growth, which again is our sole purpose on this plane, we will have many more opportunities. Have no fear, God will give you another situation appropriate for developing these skills and determining which choice to make again, maybe really soon. The more wisely you choose, which usually translates to making the most difficult choices voluntarily, the more situations come up from which you can choose. Depending upon your particular lesson plan, they may get easier, or they may be harder – geared toward your personal growth plan and assessment. Also depending upon your directives, they may come faster or slower. That is God's decision and God's job. Some things are planned into your lifetime, and some things you have control over. Choose wisely when you can, to make the most spiritual progress.

You might skate by an entire lifetime choosing door number one, and live to a ripe old age, and God might allow it without one little speck of worry. However if you constantly choose to see things only in the manner in which you want to in this lifetime and not challenge yourself, your decisions that all look like the number threes (hard decisions) of an easy lifetime, will operate as the number ones, or worse, of the later lifetime. In other words, it will be quite difficult in comparison, and the distinctions between materially easy, materially slightly difficult, and materially quite difficult of an easy lifetime, turn into materially hard, materially very hard, and materially oh good grief almost impossible, of perhaps the next lifetime. The resulting lifetimes are in correlation to how much work you put into raising your spiritual vibration.

For comparison sake, if you don't make the effort to connect to spirit world and learn this stuff, the decisions of an easier life may continuously present themselves on a daily basis to resemble:

1 - choosing a second home or donating time to an orphanage or not (door number one);

2 - buying a yacht or giving to charity (door number two)

3 - avoiding family members that genuinely need your help or volunteering to replace a wing of a day care center that has been

damaged by a tornado and has no insurance, but they will dedicate a room to you (door number three)

As opposed to your choices in the more difficult lifetime resembling:

1 – choosing whether or not to abort a child because you can't feed it, as opposed to putting it up for adoption or selling it (door number one)

2 – while still poor, you along with your husband figuring out how you will make a living having each been born blind, or trying to survive as blind people who have to make a living and work through one of you having bi-polar disorder in order to care for your younger sister who was abandoned at birth by your parents because she is also deaf/mute, in addition to her blindness.

3 - in addition to blindness, you are living in a country where in order for the rest of your family, including your sister to live, you must decide if you will prostitute your 13 year old nephew, or drown your newborn

The harder you work at making the more difficult spiritual choices this time, the less karma you will have to work off the next time – or think of it as make-up work, though there will still be other lessons. Choose easy all the time now, get hard all the time the next time, or in a future life. Remember, material or corporeal does not always mean money, but might mean requiring time, effort, patience, etc. Though there are some "vacation" lives, where people really are taking a break because they have had such hard lifetimes maybe the last 10 or so, generally speaking, if everything is too easy, and you keep it that way always choosing door number one, you aren't raising your vibration and frequency very much. A chart might look like this:

Corporeal/Material easy
= Spiritually low vibration/growth
Corporeal/Material medium difficulty
= Spiritually medium vibration/growth
Corporeal/Material high difficulty
= Spiritually high vibration/growth

With this in mind, it does not behoove one to choose what seems like the easy route all the time, unless you want to return to this plane again facing far more difficult lessons.

This brings me to an obvious point about my own not so easy life which, of course, I've asked about. Almost all of my life decisions begin at hard and go to impossible. So what was I in past lifetimes? I am 89 lives incarnate and all have been experienced on this planet. I was male 48 times and female 41 times. The reason my life is so difficult this go round is in part because of the progression I made into part two of my lessons, and in part because I had more than one lifetime in which I was a purely selfish being who thought only of herself. I took another woman's husband and allowed her and her children to starve to death. I also have had previous life situations in which I could have chosen to help relatives in need and did not. I have done more harm to elderly people in earlier incarnations by taking their money and being mean to them than was necessary or reasonable. In the 8th century, I was a mean master of a household and abused my servants. Geez! Talk about a slow learner.

I'm a gem, aren't I! So in this life, I am experiencing the following: hard work without appropriate recognition or pay (to some extent); numerous relationship and spousal difficulties; a life in which I will need to care for people whom will not appreciate this care or really show enough love or financial help when I need it in the manner I should be able to expect it from family and that being husbands mostly (though I've been granted incredibly loyal parents, sister, child and friends, thank goodness). These results are in response to the less than desirable things I choose to do in my past lives. In part, I have to deal with them because I have worked through so many other negative issues in this life. These are remaining issues, and I am finally ready to understand them now.

Of the past, most recent 22 lifetimes, I have made more choices from the most difficult group in order to change my karma and overcome the set of circumstances derivative of my past indiscretions. Because of that, I have been given many of these lessons in one lifetime because if I can survive this lifetime, I will have made a graduation of sorts, and am ready to concentrate on new themes. Thus far, I am ahead of schedule and doing well. My increasing level of endurance is seeing me through. If I don't tire and stay at a higher vibrational level more times than not, I will make a breakthrough and be ready for experiences in other worlds. Apparently, I got tired of repeating the same mistakes over and over again, and decided to buckle down and choose door number three consistently.

This is what I've been told:

There is a pesky little mechanism that even the most diligent, hopeful and determined individuals must work through that rises up when we least expect it, and takes over even when we are well intentioned. I call it the "nonsensical loop of repetitive behavior."

Remember, by virtue of the fact that we are here on this planet, we are struggling in the spiritual genius arena. To complicate just trying to navigate all the things that we have to figure out, we also have to deal with our own bad habits that being part of this society seems to perpetuate. Because we are caught up in the workings of an individualistic society (if you live in the U.S.A), it becomes very hard to stop doing what we want to do. This is true even when our choices are not good for and ultimately do not work for us spiritually. I suspect this is true partially because we don't fully understand how we are connected to the rest of the world. We've been fed this nonsense that we are alone, and therefore only affect our immediate families and are separate from the rest of the world. So not true, but we will talk about that in the "triangle theory" later.

For the moment, we need to remember that we are always connected to God by an energy string that keeps looping between us and Her at all times. It is not a one-way thing, but a circling connection sort of like a giant bicycle chain, with each lesson being represented by a link. Those links are adjusted by God according to the manner in which we learn the lessons. Many of the links are different variations of the same lesson. As we get one lesson, She removes the repetitive links as they are no longer needed, and replaces them with more complicated lessons/links. If we don't get the lesson the first link pertains to, we will see a similar lesson again that looks just a little different, and so on.

So when we forget that we are connected and act as if we have complete autonomy, that connection automatically snatches us back into to some sort of eventual lesson to counteract the one we just ignored so we get it again in another form. If we are bright enough to recognize the lesson and are determined enough to do what we must to break the bad habit and learn new behavior, we never need to repeat that lesson again. If not, we create the "nonsensical loop of repetitive behavior", and if we are real slow, God might add in a few more similar links in hopes that we get tired and stop the offending, (dare I say?) retarded behavior. If we seem to be doing the same thing over and over again, we just aren't getting the lesson, and we are causing the loop return because of our refusal to learn. God has all the patience in the universe, so either we get it this time, or we get it later.

Astoundingly, the most common reason for this behavior is pure arrogance. We simply do not believe that God is this interactive, and we do not believe that we can't just do what we want! We are a slow group of folks, a slow group. And I have obviously been one of the bandleaders, still am from time to time, but I'm trying to keep it to a minimum as much as possible.

There is another concept imbedded within this tendency that causes most of us problems. That is being suckered into other people's repetitive, forced non-growth patterns. We get suckered again, sometimes, because we believe that kindness is always goodness, and goodness is the point of this lifetime – to be good, versus being evil. This is a hard misconception to break if you believe in the good and evil format, as opposed to growth as the primary directive format. In fact this book will have no validity for you if you can't allow that concept of good versus evil to leave your thinking. This may only seem like nonsense.

The misguided pursuit of goodness dictates you must put up with dysfunctional people who choose to stay that way because they will not change, they will not surrender their massive wills, and they will not let go of the hold they have on everyone else's life so that they can remain dysfunctional. If this is the case, then you willingly prevent your own growth. By attempting to aid, comfort and assist a person who is unwilling to grow, you have given them permission to stop any progress you might make as you turn your life over to them for stagnation.

Usually, these people make you tired. They generally look very docile and may seem quite innocent and abused. In fact, they are empowered, and fall into the malicious group bordering upon evil/misguided because they are so self protective and self involved, that they don't care if you go down with them, as long as they get to stay in their comfort zone, and "look" like they are good. They often do many good things, but they do not meet their life's goals--growth. They will prevent your growth too, which is fairly evil. Imposition of will, to the point of destroying another person's will is quite misguided.

If you are trying to stay on track and want to grow, these people, no matter how much you love or want to help them, must be avoided at all costs if you mean to live in a state of forward movement. They are not hard to recognize. They are usually whiners, super emotional, always feel that someone is trying to do something to them or take something from them, they are very concerned with others at work who are trying to undermine their authority, their time, their money, their self- esteem, they cry easily, they never have a lover who appreciates them no matter what the person does, they always have a relative who doesn't appreciate them, they are often spoiled, and they may or may not be materially functional. The more time you devote to their insanity, the less productive you become. They almost always view themselves as victims and will do incredibly bizarre and unreasonable things to protect themselves. These actions actually make them predators as they take away the rights of others, and they never own up to any of this if it is pointed out to them. If you point it out, they claim you are abusing them - and they are relentless in all of this. They are an incredible amount of work, though they seem to always act like that is the last thing they want. Sometimes they are difficult to identify because on the face of things, they seem very supportive of you, until you analyze their actions over a period of time. Then holes appear and inconsistencies become apparent.

The biggest indicator of this type of person is they almost always choose door number one, because all else is too hard. These people usually never choose door number three, and you might be able to count the door number twos on one hand. You are usually the kind ear who can help them through their most recent on-going problem. In reality, they are sucking up your life and will, to remain stagnant while living in defiance of their own spiritual directives. In addition, they usually stack the information so that you only get part of the picture, so it is always slanted in the manner they think will allow them to remain the same, unchallenged.

These kinds of activities keep their vibrational level lowered, even if they counteract this with a high vibrational level activity like seemingly selfless charity work. Usually they can't maintain any selfless pursuit consistently, or with the right attitude, but primarily as a superficial form of spiritual insurance, so they are in a constant vibrational war with themselves. And so are you if you are too closely involved with the daily operations of these people. Remember, our purpose is about energy, and light and trying to reach the same level as God eventually. These people may as well throw a bucket of water on your light!

Thus they are preventing you from living up to your greatest spiritual potential as well. Additionally, you are allowing them to force you into a state of looped repetitive behavior each and every time you stand too close to them. Their insistence on doing what they want, instead of obviously what God wants and their lesson plan, forces them into spiritual retardation, and your refusal to set yourself free forces you into spiritual retardation as well. The best thing you can do for them and yourself is not be the crutch that they constantly depend upon while they live in the pseudo fears and perceived abuses (as they are seldom valid at all) that consume their lives (and thus yours). Run like the wind so you can meet your spiritual goals. This anvil tied to your ankle will not allow it. Maybe then, they will stop pulling you into their spiral of spiritual destruction. They usually need a co-dependent person to reach their height of retardation.

Sometimes, if you are sincerely true and pray and stay very close to God, if you cannot handle detaching yourself from this type of person because of your own lack of understanding, struggles, co-dependence or whatever, but genuinely seek God's help and are sticking to all other things that will make you grow spiritually, God may step in and help. Let me give you an example:

I have a friend who is very much like what I have described above. All spiritual lessons are difficult for her because she is so resistant. Until recently I have been her number one co-dependent. I care a lot about her, and I keep feeling that if I listen and talk things through, she might find her way to real change and stop some of the things she does that are clearly repetitive, resistant and wreak of massive spiritual retardation.

We have had many incidents in which I told her something that should clearly be in confidence. She has told or let this information slip, or somehow let it get back to the person involved. It never seemed vicious, but it was always inconvenient. Apparently not to do so appears to be, in her mind, a restriction of her rights as a human being. We have had numerous conversations about this, and I long since stopped telling her sensitive things. But we have been close for a while, and so after much talk, she has put a lot of effort into being more discreet. The fact that she knows very little because I don't say much makes it better. At the root of this somehow is the spoiled belief that the world operates like she thinks it should, and therefore she just plain and simply does not get it. She doesn't want to. It isn't important to her because it would require that she must operate differently.

One day we were discussing messages from God and how they work, and that they seldom do what we think, but are designed to accomplish what She means to happen. I told her that I had done a third party reading through someone for a woman who was spiritually attuned, but gave no name. This reading was not particularly favorable and was, in fact, quite harsh. As an aside, I've noticed that the more able you are to connect to the other side, the less flowery the language and abrupt the message. Hers was that. The woman went ballistic and was quite unhappy and questioned who I might be, considered me to be abusive and a fraud. However the message spoke directly to how she did her readings and the state of arrogance she was falling into. In some ways, she had forgotten she had no power except through God--and none on her own. I tried not to give too many details. The end result of this story was that within six months, the woman completely changed her life. I saw her, and because she didn't know I was the person who had given the reading, she was quite sweet. She had lost weight, looked completely different, lighter, laughed more often than I had ever known. It was obvious God knew what to do for her!

At the end of this story, which for me was about how God operates, my resistant friend asked if I was talking about so-and-so, and named her by name. I had forgotten that she knew this other woman casually, and given the history of her being unable to keep her mouth shut in these types of situations, terror struck in my heart. I immediately went into damage control mode. I try my best not to lie, as it lowers your vibrational level. I also hoped she had the maturity to deal with this situation as I would not want to betray the trust of a person, and thought I had protected her while still imparting the information. But some cases don't go so smoothly. Often, the people, not the lesson, are the point for individuals operating at this vibrational place and in this state of resistance.

I acknowledged that it was this person, but that my friend must understand how important it was for her to never, ever act like she knew this information, and I was sorry that I had betrayed the woman's unspoken, unknown trust in this manner. I asked that she promise that she would simply forget this, and never speak of it again. She promised, and I know her heart was in it; however, she has been in a state of spiritual resistance so long and so thoroughly, that she does not incorporate this understanding into her being. Therefore, it is unclear what will actually happen, no matter what her mental intent. The spirit is not fully engaged, so it's a free-for-all with people caught in the nonsensical loop of repetitive behavior.

A few months later, I was talking with this friend and she said she sent another woman to my website for a reading. She told me she thought I could help her friend and that my readings were about spiritual growth, which this woman was seeking. The woman had heard of the other spiritually attuned woman who had changed her life, and asked if that was who it was. My friend said, quite proudly, "No, she is the person that that woman goes to for readings." There was a sense of pride in her voice, as she felt she was speaking highly of me.

I was nearly speechless, but figured that if I focused on it she might try and fix it, which would be infinitely worse. She didn't understand what a betrayal it was for me to have said something to her in this case, even unwittingly (make no mistake it was a dual lesson from God) and she didn't understand what a short trip it was to figure out it was me, since the woman seldom had readings from other people. It's not like she would miss this one. She tried it for the right reason, and she got the right answer. My friend went right on in the conversation and, to this day, probably never figured out what might be wrong, or that anything actually was wrong with her telling her other friend this information. She can't acknowledge this error because to do so means she will have to actually hear other people, and grant them rights, which she doesn't often do. The world operates like she thinks, and that is all there is to it. She doesn't pay that much attention to what else goes on around her because if she did, she'd be forced to change, and that is not acceptable to her at this point in her spiritual development. She talks a good talk, but she doesn't walk the walk. But I do adore her other wonderful qualities, and she has many.

I was mortified! I hung up the phone, sat down on the bed and cried and prayed. I love this friend, but she is exhausting. I asked God if this would ever change, and if my friend would ever get these very basic concepts. He answered that I should have known she wouldn't understand as she does no work to make sure she gets these concepts because she does not want to. Therefore, the lessons do not stick despite repeated, dire consequences to her and those around her. I asked for help with this situation because I only felt like I, or maybe we would be caught up in this nonsensical loop for the rest of our lives. I did not think I was able to alter this pattern, and she obviously did not want to. I asked for God's guidance. She said She would help.

Four months prior to this incident, I was told that if this friend and I didn't change this unhealthy pattern in which we operated, and if I didn't stop getting stuck in her patterns of non-growth and if she didn't put more effort into growing, we would be separated. I gave her the readings that said this, and I had many warnings. I was told to stop coddling her. I tried to comply, but I found this very tough to do because she went straight for whining, or mean and nasty--neither of which I handle well. We had two differing agendas. Mine was growth, though her behavior overwhelms me and I am forced into stagnation because I don't handle her personality well and therefore allow myself to thwart my own personality. Her agenda is to stay the same, though in her deepest heart, I'm sure she wants something else – to grow. But she is too attached to the repetitive behavior syndrome.

Two weeks after my prayer, she was no better and the whining and the complaining continued. I didn't realize it until later because I think I am strong as an ox, but talking to her made me physically tired. At any rate, we were having an unrelated conversation, and I tried my tough love stance of not coddling her. I was more blunt than usual when she said something nuts, and I responded with, "Look, I just finished talking to one crazy person. There must be a rule somewhere that says you are only forced to talk to one crazy person per hour." I was really not that serious, but I did get off the phone.

She would not speak to me for days. When I tried to communicate with her by e-mail, she went into her pitiful/nasty mode, and said that I was hateful to her and obviously didn't care about her. This comes from a person who will say things to cut people to the quick, undermining their self esteem in ways I wouldn't begin to think about saying. Her level of playing the pitiful victim astounded me. Her response was way over the top, and totally inappropriate for a woman who had told me once that she was shaped like a brick house, and I was shaped like an apple. We both weigh about the same, and I am three inches taller than her. I would not say that to an enemy (much less a friend) for fear of what it might do to them at their core, or what it might do to me vibrationally. Self-delusion has a prominent place in resistance equaling spiritual retardation. The fact is, we are both too fat, period, but apparently only one of us is really clear about that.

Self-absorption is another trait of a resistant spirit, looped in repetitive behavior. Self-absorbed people are seldom in touch with truth. They can rearrange it to fit their specific needs quite neatly, even though they seldom recognize this tendency. This "rearrangement" of course is no longer truth. Truth is not your version or mine. We may have interpretations that are yours and mine, but truth is truth. Our understanding of it may change, but it remains essentially unchangeable.

In my friend's case, she can see truth quite clearly in some subjects, and not at all in others. I think this is a product of actually attempting to grow in some spurts, but unlike anyone I have ever seen, if the growth gets uncomfortable, she will sabotage it quickly returning to square one immediately. Usually people only do it in a couple of areas in life. She will trash nine or ten areas of growth quickly in order to go back to the familiar. She is a fascinating example of this phenomenon because she doesn't blink an eye at losing ground in order to return to safety when too much change is afoot. Most people don't like working hard and then losing ground. It doesn't seem to faze her, though of course she says differently. Still, the proof is in the pudding.

Her refusal to talk to me went on for about two weeks before I finally figured out that this had nothing to do with me or her. This was the fulfillment of God's promise to help. I had asked for help because I was inept at dealing with her, and God had delivered. When I asked for confirmation about the situation (the more you understand about these kinds of operations, the less information that is volunteered, and you have to ask) I was told that I was doing legitimate work to grow, and she was not. She would not be allowed to pull me off my path because she didn't want to really grow, but only pretend that she is was involved in the growing process. And that's the way it works.

Since that time, my friend and I have been allowed to talk a little, but I'm not allowed to speak to her too often, and now I know why. Without the daily conversations with her, I feel like a different person, and several people have commented that they see a difference. I am not tired, I am meeting new people, thinking in new ways about a number of things, I don't feel as if I am in a combat zone, and the most important thing I know is that I am not invincible and cannot let people who don't want to grow take up that much space in my world. I pray for her everyday in hopes that she will want to grow, as I miss the spirit I know she can be, and is sometimes. But, I don't miss the one she chooses to be too much of the time. I cannot. It is too detrimental to my well-being. I am working to move to a higher vibration that will allow me to handle her energy better.

So, at the moment in the context of this book, I am the poster child for why one might not want to choose door number one too often. I also have strong examples of how a spirit attempting to grow should not burden itself with the energy of one who does not want the same thing in earnest. That interaction will pull you down. However, many, many obstacles are in the way to clear spiritual thought that will lead to rational, non-repetitive behavior. One of the biggest is the condition of your spirit when it gets here, and how it comes to be that way.

CHAPTER SEVENTEEN
THE LIGHTS, THE GRAYS AND THE DARKS

When we arrive on this plane, we come in sizes and shapes, spiritually speaking. There are three primary categories with variations within each category. These are generalizations. I have done readings for people who are way outside of these norms, but that is rare.

LIGHT SPIRITS

Light Spirits come to this plane with a Guardian Angel, a spirit who no longer has to return to this particular plane as it has successfully completed all its work here. Its work on the other side is not complete yet, and we, the people for whom it is charged with our physical and spiritual protection, are a primary part of its tasks. Lights also have at least one Spirit Guide. There may be more; however, the purpose of the Spirit Guide is to assist us in processing information and making wise spiritual decisions. It also protects us from spiritual impairments which might keep us from making sound spiritual decisions, if we listen and don't override it. I have one Guardian Angel, and two primary Spirit Guides, one of whom I am in the most communication. The other is new to me, and we have not established as much of a personal relationship.

Lights therefore, with all this help, seldom make mean spirited spiritual decisions if they are listening and paying attention. If they do make misguided spiritual decisions, they may fix it quickly, and are usually in such turmoil that they are barely able to function. If this situation arises, they struggle and fight to stay sane until they remove themselves from negative influences and right themselves again. You can usually discern a Light Spirit more by how it views bad behavior, than whether or not they have or live bad behavior, because it is almost impossible to know the nature of their tasks on this plane. You have to listen to how it feels about things to distinguish it, because sometimes it can be just as misguided as a Dark Spirit, or a Gray and do horrific things, but the examination is in how they feel about that behavior, and what they do to get out of the negative situation and fix it.

A Light Spirit who is on course usually chooses door number three often. The Light Spirit who is off course chooses door number one the most. Our task (as I am a Light as well) is to remain on track, because often, we are given unusually difficult burdens to test us on a continuous basis.

GRAY SPIRITS

The Grays are the teeterers, and are almost always spiritually confused from moment to moment. They struggle very, very hard to stay on an even keel, and make it about half of the time, depending upon how often they choose door number three. Grays have a Guardian Angel, and usually one Spirit Guide. They fight huge battles with themselves, and can change from one day or one moment to the next spiritually speaking. They are usually the people who say things like "well that's in your opinion" or "I'm confused", or "I don't know why nothing can go my way", because they are always trying to hold some ground for fear of losing themselves. They are almost always in internal conflict, and they usually cause everyone else conflict as well.

Grays in turn do some incredible good for those around them. When they are good, they are usually very, very good with terrific examples of kindness. But, they also wreak havoc with not the worst acts, but the ones that cause the most chaos and dysfunctional states of being to themselves and those around them in almost equal proportions. They may remain in this chaos until they become determined to let go of the confusion and work hard at spiritual growth. My friend who has trouble not repeating things, no matter how much she demands that I act as if she has this skill down, is a Gray.

A lot of Grays, or Lights operating as Grays, exist in our present time because there is so much confusion, and these individuals are already in that state. If they don't work hard to avoid and not perpetuate spiritual dysfunction, they contribute greatly to it. Compounding the difficulty with this concept is the observation that so few see this, and more are resistant to taking in that information, therefore contributing to even greater confusion.

DARK SPIRITS

Darks usually come with no Guardian Angel, and no Spirit Guide. Sometimes they can have a Spirit Guide, but not the Angel. What this does is eliminate that little voice that tells you when something is wrong. They are not always bad people; however they are usually the darkest in their thinking and work hard not to let anybody know about it. Of course, some Darks actually do go over and perform some of what they are thinking. Most do not.

Often a spirit comes back Dark because they have some major thing to work through that they did not complete before. God has tried to put them in different environments, let them come with lots of help – several Spirit Guides and a couple of Angels, etc. – and still nothing has worked. So, She tries another combination, all in an attempt to get a spirit to pay attention and change the way they process information so they can grow.

In practical terms, I have found in my experiences, and through discussions with continued spirits, that an example of how each spirit might work might look like the following:

Let's say that each of the three spirits is mugged and raped at knifepoint. Their reactions to this assault might be something like the following:

The Light Spirit, if it is stable and not leaning toward the Gray or Dark side, will be glad that it made it out of the situation alive, and will be thankful. Then it is likely to try and ensure that it does not have another situation like that happen to it again. It will safeguard itself, it might work to make the area safer; it may do community work to make sure it doesn't happen to others, it may work to make sure that if possible, that assailant is not able to do that again. It may even go so far as to find a way, if it is safe, to help that person who assaulted it, to discover a method to rid him or her of such horrible behavior, if he or she is willing. If it has a flash of anger, it usually gets over it fairly quickly, and it does not dwell on such.

The Gray Spirit is more likely to go into a "why me" response, whether it admits it or not. It will stay in an anger mode too long, and teeter upon dysfunction and depression. If it is confronted with the guilty person, it is usually venomous, and it holds onto that for far too long, hampering its own spiritual progress. It has difficulty letting go, and may go back and forth between hating the person and wanting revenge and feeling pitiful and helpless, to feeling empowered and proactive and wanting to make forward moving spiritual progress. It will spend an inordinate amount of time trying to make sure that it is safe, long past the point of reason, and still may never feel safe enough again. It will invariably make others participate in its madness by requiring that pity parties take place, or that people know that they should coddle it because it has been unduly damaged.

The Dark Spirit may outwardly or secretly give in to a seething kind of rage and hatred that is likely to stay with it forever, or at the very least if it is working on their spirituality, too long. It will never forget this incident if it does not check itself. It will judge all others who share any similarities to the offender by the actions of this one person. It will feel it has proof that the world is evil, so that any evil it might do in the future is only par for the course and it is justified. This may be conscious, or subconscious and reveal itself in its behavior or, if it is very controlled, its beliefs only and not its actions toward others. It will stew in a dark place in its heart and may become self-destructive and fall into bad habits that don't attempt to alter their moods, but uses this anger in order to maintain a darker mood. It will feel sorry for itself and know that it has been wronged and may, in turn, want to wrong others. It may also have visions and/or fantasies about hurting the person, or other people in response to this incident, and it may actually act on it. If they are working on themselves consistently, it will not do any of this, but will work just as hard to get rid of these feelings, and so you may hear them say things like "I stay in church every Sunday and Wednesday night, so I don't have to kill somebody."

Bear in mind that it takes effort to lose ground if you come with a Light Spirit, and effort to gain ground if you come with a Dark Spirit. Either way, the point of this life is to work at being your best spiritual self, and the incident that has happened, is only a test presented by God to see if you will work to gain, or fight to maintain. You can go either way with all tests. God's job is to put the tests before you, and our job is to gain spiritual ground and grow, and not simply maintain and stay stagnant. This is true for Lights as well, as there will always be some area of concern that we must all work on, from which we will learn.

We gain spiritual advancement if we work hard to do so, and we lose it when we refuse to move forward. The catch is that we go back home, or take an exit point, if we don't try hard enough and appear to be in danger of regressing. But, we also go back home if we have done exceptionally well, progress and learn all of our assignments for this lifetime. However, only God knows what that gain/loss scenario looks like, because it is not a good versus evil kind of school, but a points-gained, and points-lost situation in which our lessons are the key. What looks like loss on one side (death) may be a gain depending upon the big picture of your life. Again, the concept to keep in mind at all times is that we don't run anything. Only God does. All we can have control of is how much effort we put into growth.

The manner in which you deal with the lessons and the choices you make accordingly are the things that make for progress. Remember, good and evil are tools to achieve growth and not the ultimate on this plane. They are primers for us to learn bigger lessons. Keeping all of this in consideration, when a situation keeps coming into your world (especially if they are repetitive), you must consider which of these spirits you might be. This will help you know how hard you must work not to fall into the "nonsensical loop of repetitive behavior."

You must also consider that other people are trying to promote their own agenda, and they are one of these three spirit forms as well. If they are prone to greater struggles, like in the case of Dark Spirits because they have little help, then they are even more likely to pull you off your path of progression if they not working at their own spiritual growth. If they are Grays, and you are confused, they will likely confuse you more unless you are aware of this and work to combat it. If you are Light, but have an extremely difficult road, you still have to be careful because it is easy to be distracted if you do not put your primary contact and work with God first, and allow the other Spirit types to take up too much of the time you need to move forward.

How you navigate these issues and what sort of progress you make is in part a product of your position within your Study Group. Your success within your Study Group will determine when you will take an exit point. If you are stubborn and always covering the same material you are probably behind in your Study Group, or vice-versa. Alternately, you may be ahead of your group and either moved to another Study Group so you can learn faster and more, or it may be time to exit, and get into a whole new kind of school. In order to understand how best to recognize the complications of your particular lesson plan, when for the most part you don't have direct contact, we must understand the significance, breadth, magnitude, and challenges you have because of your decided spiritual capacity along with the skills and shortcomings of your Study Group.

CHAPTER EIGHTEEN
SPIRITUAL CAPACITY

It is not difficult for people to understand the concepts of physical capacity. An athlete trains, runs, eats a certain way and eventually he begins to build greater lung capacity, endurance, and physical aptitude or capacity. This improvement takes place even if he has only moderate natural talent in his chosen sport, thanks to his great discipline and commitment to improvement.

The same goes for mental capacity. A person may be reasonably bright, but if they study and work hard, and stay open minded they can build their mental capacity beyond what might be originally expected. They may learn to actually operate at a rate higher than what might be the norm of 10 to 20% of one's brain aptitude or capacity.

Why should that concept not be the same for spiritual capacity? If you believe any of what has been said in this book, I am an example of that very point. If a person works hard and focuses and prays a lot, that person can build upon whatever spiritual gifts and aptitude they came with to this plane. That in fact, I contend, is the point of our existence. It seems irrational to think that a person who is waging war, trying to control others, abusing children, or killing others is operating at a high spiritual capacity. Activities such as developing systems of separatism and elitism in order to dominate instead of uplift other human spirits, or using belief systems such as religion for personal monetary gain, or to create spiritual elitism that alienates others, are surely indicative of low level spiritual activity.

Hence, the activities to increase spiritual awareness require the same type of exercises as the physical and mental capacity exercises. We must raise our vibrational levels in order to operate at a higher frequency. We need no mediator in order to connect directly to the source. In fact, the mediators we have, priests, preachers, monks, astrologists, psychics, and the like, should only be guides who can show us methods to better connect to God on our own. If they are telling us anything other than that, beware. Some are misguided, but some also know this instruction that people must have a mediator, is inaccurate.

Consider the systems like birth and death. Understand this, we come into this life in direct conjunction with God, we leave this life in direct conjunction with God. Therefore, it is illogical to think that God would force us individuals go through another person in order to connect to It for guidance. Meanwhile, we operate by this "string" or energetic thread connection directly to God, the source from which we derive spiritual energy. Is it rational to think that we must travel through a priest in order to reach the entity who is already connected to us and vastly interactive in our lives? Not hardly. So if you are feeling that in order to know what God wants from you, you must find out from someone else, you clearly are not spending enough time trying to connect to the source to find out for yourself. Worse yet, maybe you fear that you cannot connect on your own. Connecting with God on our own is possible; however, it must be done correctly with reverence, respect and humility.

Perhaps the reason a person has fear is because that person is a Dark Spirit, and does not "hear" that inner voice, which is probably their Angel or Guide anyway, since these entities are easier to hear. Whatever reason God chose to bring you back in that particular state, the fact remains that it is still your duty to attempt to connect. If you are diligent, you might change your spiritual status and have more help. If you begin to truly get the lesson, your spiritual status is very likely to change, even if you have to work especially hard.

Similarly, maybe you have fear because you have convinced yourself that you are not capable of making this connection on your own, but must have a person intercede on your behalf. This mistaken belief is often perpetuated through parental, community or religious teachings. If this is what you believe, then it merely means that you have yet another obstacle between you and God that you will have to remove in order to have the strongest connection possible. Don't get me wrong, a person with a stronger connection than yours can assist you, but that person cannot do it for you, at least not on a permanent basis. Such a person might be able to help you remove negative energy that has come in assault mode as either your test, or because you drew it, but they cannot sustain a lifetime of spiritual growth for you. This task is your job.

This means that a person who is going to church for forty years, listening to a preacher, but doing nothing more to connect to God is not growing. That person has turned over the task of increasing their spiritual capacity to a third party who is not responsible for their growth. Each person is accountable to God, therefore each person must interact with God directly. The minister will not be answering for your indiscretions and have the lesson plan adjusted according to your growth needs. Nor will he be allotted your spiritual growth and shorten his reincarnations on this plane for the positive efforts you have made to increase your spiritual aptitude. Considering this, any relationship with a mediator must be put into proper perspective. They are guides, short-term at that, to help us understand how to increase our own connection to God. No one else can live our spiritual lives for us, and no one else can decide how far we will progress in this lifetime. It is our job to go as far as we can without resistance and without fear.

I do want to caution anyone embarking upon this level of communication. If you approach attempts to connect directly with God with arrogance, you are likely to cause yourself more energetic problems than you want or can handle. If you do so without protection prayers, and really do open gateways, there is no telling who you might be talking to. Please make sure to remain respectful at all times of the awesome power that is the Creator, and treat such communications as such.

CHAPTER NINETEEN
SETTING SPIRITUAL GOALS

Another mechanism is the tricky limited projection of spiritual goals. Because we generally operate under the misnomer that we are material beings first, we often listen to the material limits people put upon themselves more intently. I had a business partner who perceived himself as growing up poor, thus his self-imposed material limits guided all of his activities.

In fact, his father was a skilled tradesman and his mother a service worker, both of whom brought in decent working class salaries. They had four children and barely owned their own home. In contrast, my father was the only person working for money in my house, with five children, two of whom he put through college while he also returned to school full time. My mother took care of our small home, which they paid for with cash. They worked and saved for years, moved us to a foreign country for three years to live when I was a child, and we went on vacation every summer. My mother made our clothes and for six years nobody worked except during the summers and part-time on weekends (for my sisters in college). But I never thought we were poor, and I know we could not have had as much money as my business partner's family did. What was different?

Perception. He decided that he had limits, so he did. He was brilliant in his field, but told me early in our partnership at age 30, that he wanted a Jaguar by the time he was fifty-five. He had set his material goal. I came in and attempted to implement systems that might allow him to buy that Jaguar within five years, at about age thirty-five. No matter what I did, he found a way to sabotage each and every effort after he figured out that we might actually make financial progress beyond his self-imposed material limitations.

With every attempt to live down to those limitations, he was throwing us into debt, or destroying our reputation so that we had reduced income. He tried to take things back to a comfortable state of limitations lest he reach his material goal too quickly, and then what would he do? I could see it, but I couldn't help him stop himself. I jumped ship.

He had forgotten that this is a spiritual and not a material journey and created a dim energy connection barely flickering between him and the Creator. Otherwise, he would have relaxed in the confidence that the messages in his work were divinely inspired and actually part of his spiritual directive, his true purpose and destiny. Some people find their work purpose early in life, as he did, but can't link the two. They limit their goals, making them singularly material in nature, or too low and attainable spiritually or a combination of both. This can only occur in an atmosphere of fear, without understanding that this is all God's plan and our only purpose is to relax and follow Her evident instructions. Resistance to His will always clouds purpose. Setting a low spiritual goal leaves a lot of room to get lost.

We must make our spiritual goals, like the material goals, lofty enough to provide inspiration, so we might be motivated to achieve them. Some people can't define their spiritual goals. They may figure out material aspirations, albeit fraught with problems like my partner, but few identify their God inspired spiritual goals. Often, people apply material terms to spiritual goals as well. For example, many Christian churches direct their members to tithe 20% to the church; do as the minister says, or to do charity work. I doubt that these are direct and succinct enough directives to help us achieve our highest and best self and thus true purpose. We are still trying to connect to each other through the material. It is only through our connection to the Creator that we can effectively connect to each other, and thus all substantial goals start with the Creator. The rest will occur naturally.

When setting spiritual goals, it becomes important to recognize a few things. If the goal has another person between us and God, it is not going to be proactive enough to inspire us. In other words, if you make your goal convoluted and make it something like, "I want to operate more like God and do his bidding, so I vow to attend church on Wednesdays so that I can hear the word of the Minister about how to best do that." Listen to that carefully. It is like saying that I am going to learn to sing, so I will go listen to the opera so I can be a better singer. Does that look direct enough to accomplish your goal?

If you want to talk to God with the hope of receiving guidance from Her, spend that two hours on Wednesday night talking to God! Doesn't that make more sense? If you wanted to learn to drive a car, would you do so by watching other people drive cars down the street? At the very least, you might watch them for a short period of time, but eventually, you would want to get in a car with someone driving and pay close attention. And while you might read the driver's handbook, you can't do that your entire life with no practical driving experience and expect to be able to drive.

The point is that you cannot connect to God that way either. You can read the book, whichever one you use as a guide: the Bible, the Qur'an, Bhagavad Gita, etc., but at some point, you can't watch others connect to God. You can't read about it and expect to actually grasp hold of who God is in your life, and hope to have Her be able to respond to you and you hear or feel, or see the answers. It just won't happen because you have not done the thing that will allow you to raise your vibration and thereby connect. You haven't dialed the phone up enough times to get an answer. And you sure can't connect on a regular basis if you aren't attempting to do it yourself, unless your minister moved in and figured out how to take full responsibility for your spiritual life, and somehow God allowed that. Can't imagine how that might work long term though.

The issue here is that you have set your sights much too low. Somewhere along the way, you were convinced, or you convinced yourself that these low expectations were all that were reasonable and attainable for you. Therefore they are all you will achieve.

Hence, our spiritual goals must include seeking to close the gap between us and God, allowing us to connect positively to God directly and thereby arrive at our true purpose. We should not get this twisted. This life is an energy current of which we are not the originators, nor can we affect substantial change except through the originator, like a closed circuit. In fact, it is only through God that we can connect effectively to other spirits.

CHAPTER TWENTY
THE EVIL TWINS

There are two things that keep us from making progress on the lessons God designed for us to achieve and that we must set as goals to accomplish. They are fear, the immobilizer, and stubbornness, the incapacitator. If either of these is allowed to run wild, they stop all progress. If we are to grow to become our best spiritual self, we must banish them from our thinking. That of course, is no joke since they are pervasive, and when un-checked, take over our entire being, sometimes without our consent or recognition that they are ruling.

When they are running our show, they often act in conjunction with one another. Usually, something, whether pre-designed in our lesson plan, or created by the influence of a parental lesson plan gone mad, will force us into thinking in limited terms about who we are and who we have the capacity to become. This can prove true both on the spiritual and material realms. One does not have to have the other to survive, although stubbornness cannot survive without fear. But when they operate in unison, they are formidable.

Fear gives us a false sense of who we are spiritually and either makes us feel undue limitations or undue strength and power. If not led completely by God, we are likely to determine that everyone is out to get us in some form or fashion because the world is just too unsafe. Under this mind-set we must always protect ourselves from even the slightest infraction because if not, we cannot survive it. This of course is absurd as humans are quite resilient and strong, and spirits are by definition, long enduring, and thus ultimately durable.

We are designed to weather much, so that we can live through all the lessons that we need in order to learn and grow, and if we do so well, run another universe. I have met a person who when I asked, found out that she was only 8 lives old – and believe me, she acted like it. She was a bad, obnoxious, self-serving child, even though I met her when I was a child. She never got better, and died a spoiled, mean brat as an old woman.

I have spoken to only two spirits who were more than 450 lives old. One of these old spirits was the grandmother I saw on the rocks, who officially began my intentional communication journey with continued spirits, not a chance communication, I am convinced. I've been told she is not required to reincarnate to our plane. This is an example that our journey may be long before we get to the work of doing our second training somewhere other than this plane exclusively. Our second training might take many more life measurements on the other side before we reach our ultimate goal. Since nobody has actually done that, and a new universe has not yet formed, what could we possibly be concerned about? We are spiritually invincible in the bigger scheme of things, only physically fragile.

Let me explain further: When I asked how old the oldest returned (to our plane – not planet as it could have been on other planets as well, and that's all the same to God) spirit might be, I was told that the spirit was 910 lives along. When I asked how old the oldest continued spirit or one on the other side doing their college and graduate work might be, I was reminded first that it might be more like middle school or a little less, through fifteen PhD's, and that that spirit was 10,040 lives old. Considering there is no new universe, they are still on their journey. We are babies folks, which is why arrogance, fear and stubbornness make no sense if you can put them in perspective. Yet it explains why they would be things we must overcome because only some really young children would be dealing with such low level activities, such as well . . . arrogance, fear and stubbornness.

In the case of fear, if you consider those examples as guidelines, we are not fragile, even death is not a big deal in the scheme of things, we cannot actually be destroyed, and our journey is incredibly long. With that in mind, why make it longer and harder with nonsense like fear and stubbornness? Additionally, the constant preoccupation with "the end", Armageddon, and death is really quite silly when you think about it. We do have eternal life. We just have to determine how we want to live eternally. But, we will be leaving here, and it doesn't matter who you believe in, you will be continuing somewhere else, or you will be coming back. So let's put this in perspective. The question becomes, how do you want to experience any of those options? In light, trying to find light, or wishing you knew what light was.

Back to fear. When we disconnect from the awesome power of God and the expansion of this mission that each of us is on, how can we possibly condone a system that helps throw us out of whack and retard our growth, like fear? Why would we willingly employ a system that says that we are always in danger emotionally, physically, psychically, spiritually and a host of other ways? Perhaps we want to make this journey longer, while we ignore the obvious? If you buy into this, we cannot be destroyed rather only have our progress delayed.

What can be destroyed? Our bodies? Yes. So what? They are going to wear out anyway eventually. Our figurative hearts? No. It is part of what makes us who we are spiritually. Our pride? Needs to go. It is a kindergarten tool. Our imagination? No, it can't be taken away really, though while we are learning, we might foolishly surrender it. Our ego? Yep, it is in the way of most growth anyway, so let it go and be happy. Our self-esteem? How can that leave us unless we willingly give it up, especially if you are old enough to read this book? So realistically, what does fear save, or save us from? How does it protect us, not in a foolish sense, but realistically from a spiritual standpoint? It really doesn't help us at all when you think seriously about it.

Perhaps the major obstacle to raising vibrations, and thereby strongly connecting to God is fear. Allowing fear to dictate our actions prevents the Creator/us energy exchange, thereby causing an obscure and clouded connection. Fear's operational methods are limited learning; limited goal setting, and self-inflicted overrides.

Another major obstacle driven by and similar to fear is arrogance, but it takes on a life of its own. If fear is the immobilizer, and stubbornness is the incapacitator, then arrogance is surely a massive mountain since it incorporates both of these, and adds on severe stupidity (defined as the lack of intelligence or incapacity for perceiving, learning, etc.) in its purest form. Arrogance makes you believe that you are not afraid of doing something, but instead, that you are justified in your attempts to override God's will for you. I have even heard people say that it is their God given right to do something obviously not God planned, but that's another book.

Fear triggers our inappropriate, overly cautionary behavior, preventing forward movement, and perceiving danger in mere opportunities for growth. If we give in to psyche created, unhealthy fear, (not healthy fear as exercised in activities like recognizing the danger of walking off a cliff) we riddle the road to our true purpose with potholes and roadblocks. When we push away those thoughts, actively seeking to destroy them much like the system used in the tennis ball server theory, we increase the vibrations between the Creator and us and turn on the light switch that illuminates our spiritual goal, our direction, or assigned purpose per lifetime. The first task is to identify and prevent this malady of fear.

Because fear comes in so many forms, shapes, sizes and colors, it requires constant effort to recognize and eliminate when it leaps from behind the bushes and surprises us. Depending upon our life lessons and spiritual placement during this lifetime, some spirits have an easier time because of excellent teachers who helped them understand the workings of this demon. Others are swamped, and have to work against parental and community misguidance, often spending entire lifetimes without identifying even the smallest bastions of fear that literally destroy their relationships, progress, lives, and inhibits understanding of clear, Divine inspired purpose. You can't move forward while immobilized by terror. The path is just too dimly lit.

So in our quest to get through this educational system, if fear is our guide, we fight against the obvious and implement methods that impede our movement toward our apparent goals. An especially effective method of non-growth through fear is to exercise the theory of limited learning, or "the nonsensical loop of repetitive behavior."

Ever been around someone who can't alter a particular behavior, usually apparent, recurring and causing them problems, like drug addiction, inflexible thinking, abusive relationships or self-induced physical problems? They conceptually comprehend the difficulties at hand, yet still repeat the behavior. Possible solutions come to them from all directions and in all forms, without utilization. Suddenly for no perceptible outside reason, as if a light bulb has gone off, voila, and they are ready and able to learn to do things differently. This appears to be the process of limited learning. For whatever reason, upbringing, life's experiences and the like, they willingly put a glass ceiling on comprehension of the subject because whatever loomed beyond that self inflicted limit was more frightening than what they already knew. Unfortunately, as long as this mechanism is in place, no new information seeps in, thus no new realizations can be reached, no growth can occur, and fulfilling our educational mission lays dormant until we pass God's test.

The operational mechanism for this is fear, which has then immobilized us and kept that person, or us, from doing anything other than what we already know. If we are strong willed, and most people are, even when perceived as weak, then we refuse to operate differently because the fear is too great. So we employ the other twin--stubbornness, and become unyielding to logic, unyielding to outside pressure, unyielding to truth, unyielding to the obvious, and determined to maintain our comfort zone, which by the way is not working. But that's a minor point! We don't care as long as we don't have to move into some scary, new place. So we opt for repetitive behavior, no matter how dysfunctional, so we won't have to do things that are more frightening.

I'm afraid that I have too many examples in my own world for my tastes, but apparently that is the point in part of writing this book. I'm such a good example.

For two years I've been told to write this book. For two years, I have felt totally unqualified, and for two years, I complained, whined, threw minor tantrums, hissy fits, and flat out wouldn't put the time into doing this. When God means for you to do something, it will get done, as I said before.

For the past six months, I have not been able to make a living. No freelance work actually materialized, no business opportunities come to fruition, and it has been pretty hellish. I've been working hard every day at what ought to work, which for me is more than others ever have to do. Finally I am a week from foreclosure, and everybody on the other side starting shouting at me almost, to write the book. God politely said, "You are being stubborn." I complained that I am not qualified to tell people that which I barely understand, like a school child. His response is that I'll be talking to other school children and they will understand at my same level, if they are determined to. This week, She said if you don't write the book now, since you have ignored me for so long, you are on your own with saving the house. And She means it. Yet I know, because I have had too many demonstrations now to reject the notion, that on the day I finish this book, if it is before foreclosure, which I am determined it will be, I won't lose my house. Magically, as if a miracle, while doing Its job, something will happen to stop it, God willing literally.

I still don't feel I am qualified (fear), but I'll tell you what! In five days, I've written about half of what you've read thus far, and I intend to be finished with the entire book in four more days come hell or high water! I have lollygagged and messed around for two years, but then I can write three fourths of the book in about ten days? That can only be called, without doubt, massive stubbornness! And I know better, at least in other areas that don't scare me to death.

We are all subject to this because we are not the brightest bulbs in the pack. We are too young to be that. Accept it, and do the best you can, beating down these twins whenever possible.

TWENTY ONE
TUDY GROUP

The Study Group is easy yet difficult to explain. It has been explained to me as the group of people you come in contact with. Think of it as being in school and having an inner circle of friends. There are the popular people whom everyone knows, but you don't really associate with them, except one of the girls will occasionally come sit with you during lunch. Then there are the political kids, whom though you have no immediate contact, may affect your thinking because they are always passing out fliers, or protesting, etc. All of these people and all of the people with whom each of us comes in contact, constitutes our personal Study Group. Our individual Study Group overlaps other Groups as well, so then they also become part of our Study Group - an Extended Study Group of sorts.

We are to learn from each other and support each other, or shock each other and make our destinies different because we don't want to be like a certain member of the group. Sometimes we expel ourselves from a group and move into a new group because it is moving in new directions. Other times God removes us from the group and either puts us in the dunce corner, or moves us to an accelerated class if we show greater ability. In essence, we study together, and if we learn at the same pace, we may stick together (some of us), or we move faster or slower than our peers, and we part and move in other directions, expanding our Study Group. Many of the members of our group we have been with before in other incarnations, while others are brand new to us.

Our immediate group is the Study Group. Our larger group, all the people we come in contact with can be considered Spiritual School, like fourth grade, though unfortunately, some of us remain in Pre-K, for far too many incarnations. Our goal is to learn and maintain the ability to become our best spiritual selves within, and because of The Study Group.

Apparently, each primary Study Group has access to at least one Direct, or strong Clairsentient, or Clairvoyant, so that they can get some answers from God, via Her or the spirit guides or ancestors, or Angels when they actually need and seek real answers. Some Directs or any of the Clairs, and perhaps some other communicators, are the telephone lines for a large Study Group and speak en masse. Others, like me, have a small group who has immediate access and almost immediate answers. Bear in mind that even though there are only 40,000 Directs, there are hundreds of thousands of Clairsentients and Clairvoyants who are quite accurate. Also remember that we are no smarter, or wiser, but generally we are not as resistant to change I have noticed and have been told. We are generally more flexible which helps when hearing difficult messages. We tend to be more obedient as well, but that might be because we also have clearer, swifter, and immediate corrective measures delivered upon us!

When we work well together, we should all learn from the core group, but that depends upon how open and ready for change everyone is. In certain circumstances, many people are brought together in order to accomplish or work through one thing or another. However, if two members (for example) in the group lack the maturity to work through their lesson together, then we still might not complete that lesson in this lifetime either, and may have to repeat it. Rarely, if you ask, and God is willing to find another way for one or the other of you to work though this particular lesson, She might allow you to avoid contact with an especially difficult person, if you are doing what you should otherwise.

I have a relative who falls into this category. Although there are many wonderful things about him, no matter what I do, we are never quite right, and our relationship has been unnecessarily painful. He has a massive ego, and I have had only unpleasant moments with this person for many years. He shares many of the most negative aspects of my father, and I find him unusually arrogant and avoid him completely. He's at 41 lifetimes, while I am at 89, so we are likely to see things slightly differently. Generally, he feels like a self-involved child to me, though he has very adult, responsible parts as well. I finally conceded that I have not reached the maturity level to deal with this person effectively, and I've been here with him three times including this lifetime. It doesn't feel like we could possibly be making progress, so I asked if there was a way for me not to ever have to come back and live another lifetime with him in the future. I was told that yes, it would be granted as I had learned much in the general realm of our joint lessons, and could get the rest of that class in some other form. Almost immediately, this person has all but disappeared from my life--happily so for me, and probably him too. As I said, if you are generally obedient, and ask humbly, many things might be granted if they do not conflict with God's lesson plan.

One of the things we learn from operating within Study Groups is how to play nice, and how to share, but also how to go to a parent when appropriate, and how to learn when it is appropriate. As in this case, sometimes we simply cannot handle another classmate and need help, but most often we have to learn to work things out. The spiritual methodology for that begins with prayer, but there are also energy exchanges that are physically proactive as well that can accompany prayer for the greatest impact, like the energy triangle.

Generally, we do learn from each other and we might stay together if there is still more to learn, or we might part ways. Our lessons are carefully designed by the Master Chemist to teach each person what they need individually, either from individual contact, or from the interaction of the group, or observation of the interaction of individuals of the group. Sometimes we keep in touch, and at other times we don't. These different forms of interaction within our Study Group are one more method to get us through school.

CHAPTER TWENTY TWO
THE ENERGY TRIANGLE

Generally, the more practice you put into connecting with other people, the better the relationships and the easier the communication becomes. However this does not override God's lessons. If someone in the group has something to be learned, that always takes precedence over whatever communication you might attempt. Thus, communication with a Study Group member may be difficult if it is not God's will, no matter what you do, because either or both of you may have something to learn from that experience. There may be a purpose in your having difficult relationships on a physical or ethereal plane when you attempt to go through God and not directly to the person. However, you can't go directly to the person and circumvent going through God if it is meant for you to only communicate in that manner. This can become sort of a catch 22 situation, but it is much easier to understand if you just accept the fact that God runs everything, so if something is happening other than what you thought you would see in the way of results, everything is still under God's direction.

Again, the bicycle chain connection to God is always going, circulating the energy between us and It. However when we pray for God's light, it intensifies the energy like turning on a switch. If we desire the most effective communication with another person, it is best established and has the strongest connection and greatest positive effect when we go through God. She is the originator of all things, and He uses that energy shared between us and It to reach other human (and more) spirits. That same energy then circulates through that person, back through us, and then to God. This creates an energy triangle: beginning with us, to God, to the other person, back to us and then back to God.

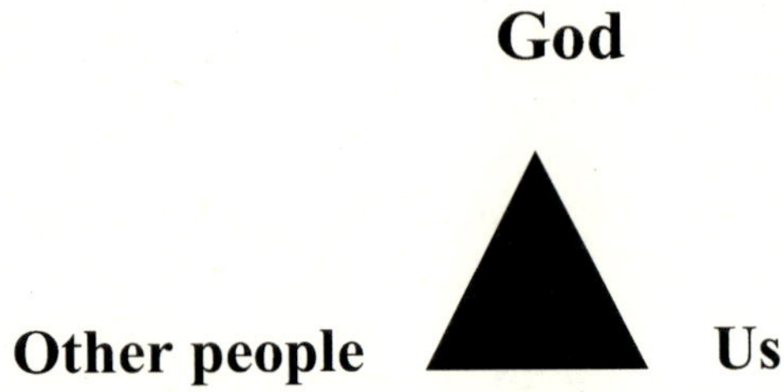

To accomplish this transference of energy, we will use what I call Stage One of the Triangle. The way it works for me (and others to whom I have taught the method I was trained to use), is to close your eyes, and request that God please allow you to be part of Its brilliant light and energy. When you make the request, concentrate on sending the request through your Third Eye, which is an energy entry/exit point, located about an inch above your eyebrows in the center of your forehead. That is where you will see the image of an eye if you do this correctly.

After you've made the request, you should experience the sensation of your skull opening up in the top of your head, from one side of your head to the other as you become more practiced. Sometimes you have to hold on to your seat, because the sensation can be a little overwhelming at first. I have read that it is an opening of your crown chakra if you want to study the phenomena. You should feel a surge of energy moving from both the top of your head and through your third Eye, and up toward infinity. As time goes on and with practice, you can feel it stop at a definite point that is God, though Its location will seem vague. I'm sure this is because of our limited perception, because I have been told that God's connection to us is constant, and ongoing, therefore instantaneous. So this system is a formality that forces the connection to become much stronger because through this exercise, our connection becomes much more willing and intentional. This intentional intervention strengthens our contact. The intensity of the energy exchange may induce slight headaches in the beginning. The more you practice the easier this connection becomes. If you are doing it right, you might also get sleepy. In the beginning, anytime a person attempts to communicate with any continued spirits, they are likely to get very tired or sleepy.

Once the connection is fully established and you feel a strong connection between you and God, you move to Stage Two. At this point of the Triangle, you should humbly request that He please send light to whomever it is that you want to help find the strength to stop some offending behavior, like smoking, drinking, raging, drugs, warring, etc. This does not have to be someone you know personally, but anyone that you can visualize clearly. You can see the beam, in your inner vision, (remember that your eyes are closed) come down from the point where you felt God to be. It will be as strong a beam of light as yours to God, and you can visualize the bicycle chain between God and the person for whom you are attempting to pray and requesting light. If you are in the same room with them, they will usually start rubbing their heads, and might get sleepy or tired. When delving into such unfamiliar territory, it helps to have visual confirmation. It helps you from thinking you are crazy, and it solidifies the fact that we are connected and that we have joint work to do, as we affect each other so completely.

Once you can maintain this visual and the light is strong between you and God, and then you can hold onto the God and the person's light visualization (which by the way goes into their crown chakra as well), it is time for Stage Three of the Triangle. This step is much more advanced and may take some serious practice. While you may be able to connect with God and intensify this connection and accomplish some things, I don't recommend that you drive while participating in this connection. After much practice, I can make these connections with my eyes open and while driving, but it took about a year of concerted practice for me to get to this point. When you do stage three, please be seated in a chair, and do not attempt to do anything else. There may well be people who can do other things in Stage Three, but I can't imagine it from my neophyte state.

During Stage Three you request that the light comes back to you and clears all blockages from everyone's chakras, meaning yours and the person or persons you are connecting to through God, and that you are able to receive this light. If the other person is open, meaning not blocked, you will feel and see the light come through all of their chakras. You may envision this transfer like an electrical current as it moves through you back to God. It is not painful, but it is highly visual, and you can differentiate the chakras that the light cannot pass through on the other person because you can feel the blockages. In the places it is not blocked, the light comes back to you and into your heart chakra, (at least that is where mine comes in). Hold that as long as you can. It takes great concentration, and it will sometimes make you feel as if your head may explode in the beginning.

After some practice, and having been taught this system by God, I was also taught to break through minor blockages on another person. It is possible. I have no blockages anymore generally if I stay on top of prayers and my spiritual practices, so you have to work with God, to push the energy through another person's blocked chakras. For me, it is almost like using an energetic soft jack hammer used on city streets to break up blockages and allow the energy to flow through all chakras. Everyone's visual is different.

In the beginning I could not hold Stage Three for more than a couple of minutes. Now I can request that light be sent through and come to me, and hence back to God, completing the circuit, through five people simultaneously, and hold it for about ten minutes. Let me share a recent experience I had with Stage Three communication. The other morning, I was feeling like I truly loved the world a little more than most days. I requested that God send light to the whole world, trying to get more efficient so that perhaps we could stop some of the madness like wars and greed. I won't be doing that again anytime soon. It was a very different umbrella effect, and I suspect that God only gave me a small sampling, as I have been told that I will have to learn to send to thousands eventually. I made the request at about 6:30 a.m., and I could not hold it 30 seconds because I thought I was having a stroke. God stopped it for me because I didn't have the presence of mind to do so. Clearly this example was a lesson.

My head hurt till at about 3:00 p.m. in the afternoon, and I had to take over the counter headache drugs to stop it finally. God has said nothing about it, so I'm sure I'm supposed to think about the experience and ask some intelligent questions. I don't have any yet. I'm busy trying not to give in to fear, especially if that is what I'm supposed to do. I hope to have some intelligence plop down upon me within a week, because I also know I am not allowed too much down time without coaxing. And I don't want the coaxing at the moment as I am attempting to be self propelled and not dragged along for some of these lessons. But I do need a minute's rest occasionally lest I run down the street with my dreadlocks on fire!

My heart was in the right place, as it was not ego and feeling powerful that made me make the request, it was genuine love and concern for the world. But still, I don't want the world to kill me, and clearly I'm not ready for this new phase. The further along I get in these lessons, (as with others I have watched), the less instruction you get from God and the more She expects you to figure out on your own.

At any rate, this method is most effective if you are trying to work on spiritual aspects between you and another member of your Study Group. The longer you can hold it and the more you can perform this exercise with a pure and nonjudgmental heart, the more effective it becomes and you will see differences in the person and their particular circumstances. Sharing the "light" and energy that has been charged by God because you are concerned about the person's well being is a way to be your best spiritual self. As this is the point of us being here it is at all times supported by the Creator. It is driven by the power of intention.

I've noticed when people first learn they can positively affect other individuals by sending them light, (and there are many religions and new age doctrines that suggest and practice giving healing energy including Pranic Healing, Mahi Kari, Chios, Reiki and more), they try and go from one person directly to the other. That does have some effect, but it seems not to be as strong. I learned to operate with my mother that way as a child when I willed her to sleep. I understand now that was actually a form of energy exchange. However, it is not nearly as powerful as connecting completely through God because this Triangle system requires that you turn over the connection to God. You no longer operate this show in any form, (which you don't really anyway).

When connecting to God completely, (at least at this level and I do suspect this is still pretty low level), you are making the choice to surrender all control you might think you have for the good of the receiving being. You are saying to God you know He has better methods to help the other person, and you request that She uses you to accomplish that stronger connection of light for the good of both of you. Such surrendering is a higher form of interaction than you could accomplish alone. Does that make sense? It is the permission you give yourself to release your sense of ego and power and acknowledge that you are less powerful without God's help. That release of ego gives the action and you more power to accomplish your desired task through God. Most importantly, it is our goal and duty to attempt to connect with others positively, with God always as the intermediary, energetically speaking. In that manner, we are connecting to our best spiritual selves, and attempting to assist others in attaining their best spiritual self. The greatest good and best actions always come through God. Our act of acknowledging this through our request is a proactive way to help us stay true to our purpose.

Remember that we have individual goals, but we also have collective goals. It is not a passive wish for the good of others, it is a required act to work toward that good if we are to graduate to become our best selves. We cannot complete this quest all on our own, but we can do it better through the light of God. God expects us to actively pursue such, and when we request acts within this realm, God is most likely to assist us and heighten that energy exchange. It is a step above "begging", as so many prayers become. It is interactive involvement in the improvement of the world and our fellow beings through God's light.

Something happens when we move into greater truths. The schools of thought that work to do no harm have similar truths in the common areas of concern and teaching. These philosophies are wonderful and work well. It is the side trips humans take from these ideologies that often add in too much of our own thoughts and agendas that become dangerous. But truth is truth.

CHAPTER TWENTY THREE
MAKE UP YOUR MIND! WHO RUNS THIS SHOW?

I'd rather go all day long and then some, doing almost anything else, to avoid talking about religion, but I've been told I have no more choices on this topic. Ignoring religion leaves too big of a hole, since people seem to believe that religion really does have something to do with God. Unfortunately, religion has more to do with some people using the concept of God to control other people, and yet, there is some modicum of truth in each and every religion. That's why people flock to organized religion. We are always innately seeking truth, and we are always looking for ways to move closer to the Creator.

In order to best understand religion versus knowing God – call it spirituality, the first thing we must understand is that some things are obvious. Humans can't make earth, or flowers, or oceans, or trees. Without doubt, whoever or whatever entity or system accomplished this is in charge of this planet, and this universe. For the sake of argument, let's call that entity God, or The Divine Architect. Already, God is in charge just by virtue of the fact that She/He/It knows a whole lot more, and can do a bunch more stuff. If you agree with this, let's move on.

An entity with that much more obvious power is not likely to do what we dictate. It is much more likely that we will be doing what It tells us to do, if we are smart. If we are not, we are likely to be in conflict with God. Still, the power paradigm won't flip upside down just because we refuse to do what God tells us to do. It is much more likely that we will be on the short end of the stick.

Additionally since God is not likely to do what us meager minded humans tell It to, God surely is not likely to do our bidding when we are in conflict with Its' directives. According to my teachings and understanding, these directives include growth, love, tolerance of others, and for us to make efforts to connect to our fellow beings to learn as much as possible in order to become our best spiritual selves. We must also connect effectively with God in order to accomplish these things most efficiently. These directives contain those grains of truth in many religions, and they are the common concepts that make God and religion connected.

Considering this, war does not come into play with the God directives, so any person who tells you that we are involved in "God's " war, is misguided and lying to everyone. This kind of action does not come from God. Any book, person or doctrine that says it does is just plain wrong. This element alone eliminates many religions because they base so many of their beliefs in the misguided delusion that God not only sanctions, but initiates and supports wars in His name. This constitutes a man made and dangerous lie, and is an insult to the Creator. It just ain't happening, and it never did and never will. To claim this fallacy as a base of any religion is blasphemous. With this in mind, how many religions are actually left?

Let's examine the concept of telling God to go to war for us. Assuming God means for us to be loving and peaceful and connect to each other (as mentioned in even those same religions whose people, and leaders claim the war directive as God's dictate), but She will willingly, purposefully, not only tell us to go to war, but in some cases, lead us into battle for "His namesake"? What can people be thinking when they come up with this? According to this theory, God is going to do what we say in our little pea brained world of ideas, and not just agree to a war, but also lead us to kill other people that He expects us to connect to and love, for the good of one people over another group of people? Does any reasonable person listen to this stuff when they say it out loud? And whole stories for children have been built around this concept, and we think it makes Divine sense? Never have more incorrect manmade concepts and ideas been said and propagated for the greed and small mindedness of humankind, all which has absolutely nothing to do with God.

What about exclusion? Let's examine homosexuality for example. Consider for a moment the individual medically termed a hermaphrodite - a person with both sets of sexual organs. This person also has very different accompanying hormonal levels which impacts their entire sexual construction, makeup and point of view. A hermaphrodite is one of God's creations, as we all are, and we have already established that the rest of us don't know enough to do anything like create such a unique being. Therefore, why would any thinking individual not understand that we all exist within a range of hormonal variation between average or more common balances of sex hormones that make a man or a woman to the higher levels of hormonal variations that constitute a hermaphrodite? Isn't it just as logical that a male with higher than average estrogen levels might have more feminine interest and tendencies? Doesn't it make perfect sense that this individual might also be more comfortable being a homosexual?

Who made people? Can a person be created other than through the methods that God gave us (and presumably the new neophyte methods like cloning that scientists are working on which God is allowing because He runs everything)? If not, then you and I certainly don't have the right to think of or treat a homosexual as anything except one of God's many creations. Either you understand this or not, but you can't keep changing the rules.

God makes and controls everything or He doesn't. Which is it? We can't keep moving around to suit human insanity so people can further their own twisted agendas. God either runs everything or She doesn't, and this includes accepting all of God's creations as they are. The bottom line is this. God isn't just running things when She does what you like, She also runs things when She does things you don't like. Furthermore, He doesn't care that you don't like it, not one little bit! Any school of thought, be it religion, philosophy, etc., that dictates that one of God's creations is an abomination to God, was created by a person with truth schizophrenia--who can't decide if they or God is in charge. This situation is no different than the person who tells you that God sanctions a war. All of these examples stem from human inspired madness but are not divinely inspired information.

If you believe that God created all things then you have to believe that God created ALL things--including homosexuals and hermaphrodites. We can't just decide God's in charge when we like the results, but not in charge when we don't. Even a child can see the absurdity in that foolish reasoning. God runs this show, period. We do not tell God what to do and expect this to actually happen unless we are completely out of touch with reality and have massive egos that are out of control.

Let's talk about the other obvious exclusionary religious tactic that causes the most problems in the world and is clearly manmade and not God inspired. This teaching basically dictates, "If you don't belong to this club, you will not get to go to heaven, and you are not in line with

God." There are many versions of this theory. The small mindedness of this concept amazes me and does not make sense if we examine the statistics. How would God make this work?

According to www.adherents.com, the numbers of adherents to the world's major religions are as follows:

- Christianity: 2 billion
- Islam: 1.3 billion
- Hinduism: 900 million
- Secular/Nonreligious/Agnostic/Atheist: 850 million
- Buddhism: 360 million
- Chinese traditional religion: 225 million
- primal-indigenous: 150 million
- African Traditional & Diasporic: 95 million
- Sikhism: 23 million
- Juche: 19 million
- Spiritism: 14 million
- Judaism: 14 million
- Baha'i: 6 million
- Jainism: 4 million
- Shinto: 4 million
- Cao Dai: 3 million
- Tenrikyo: 2.4 million
- Neo-Paganism: 1 million
- Unitarian-Universalism: 800 thousand
- Rastafarianism: 700 thousand
- Scientology: 600 thousand
- Zoroastrianism: 150 thousand

Clearly, of the world's 6.2 billion (2002 U.S. Census Report) people, many are in search of an understanding of the Creator, and Her dictates for their lives. If we take Christianity as an example, can we really believe that all those non-Christians with all those innocent children in each of those other religions are doomed because they don't follow

Jesus? We are really to believe that someone great enough to make a whole universe is this petty? The insult is astounding! The notion is utterly absurd.

I asked God, who does have a real sense of humor, about this one. Her answer was "I wonder how many times I need to reincarnate Jesus around all the planets in order to save all those spirits? Since he keeps learning more with each visit, I wonder how many others like him I need to bring through the system." Point taken.

Only children could think of something this ridiculous--and they would have to be competitive, selfish, self-involved children at that. Please people, surely we can think more clearly. The only purpose in espousing this type of theory is to keep people living in fear so someone can control them. The only purpose in believing something like this is to be better than someone, and to forfeit one's responsibility for their own relationship with God. This scenario removes our right to have that direct relationship with God, and thereby exonerates us from the work it takes to earn that divine relationship. The most frightening part is that many religions have some version of institutional exclusion in their operational methodology. Folks, this has nothing to do with God. Please don't insult God like that.

There is another form of egotistical power tripping that seems to somehow have a base in religion. It might be able to occur in the absence of religion, though people who lean in this direction usually seem to also believe that God is always on their side. I'm sure that some form of spiritual competition is a big part of their thinking though certainly the foolishness of "God does what I want" is at play. Let me explain:

I have another friend who was having trouble with a neighbor on some property her family owned in another state. This person was really difficult and my friend wished ill upon that individual. The person actually died within a fairly short period of time. My friend was telling me this story a few years later and said "He and his family were so mean to us that we wished him dead, and he died."

The first time she said this, I thought she was kidding about the entire thing. She wasn't. She repeated this story a few more times over the course of about a year. I figured there was something I was really supposed to understand about this situation, since God kept putting it in front of me, so I began to pay attention. I tried to analyze my reaction to her statement. I realized that if I had ever really thought I had killed someone with my thoughts or wishes, I would be mortified and almost suicidal. She, on the other hand, was almost gleeful about the amount of power she felt she wielded in this situation.

I wondered how she thought her supposed power might happen. I know there is energy between us as humans, but unless a person went through extraordinary energy rituals with the intervention of many other folks, even the most powerful energy workers and holders might have trouble rendering someone dead. They would also probably have to call up some really dark energy to accomplish this task even then, and the victim would have to have no protection whatsoever from that kind of assault. My friend didn't mention all that work and calling up of multiple Dark spirits. At that point, I wondered if she felt that short of murdering someone, there was a way for a person to die that was more in her hands than God's hands. That's when I realized that in her mind, God had nothing to do with this situation. She believed she controlled the situation completely and was powerful enough to make it happen. The only other alternative given how close she felt she was to God is that she thought that God had killed somebody for her. That's when I got frightened--mostly for her.

I began to realize how out of touch with reality she was in relation to God, the world, her own importance (or lack thereof), and how little she understood that relationship. This interchange occurred a few years before I was fully clairaudient, so I had to work it out on my own without full assistance from continued spirits. I began to realize that my friend was, in essence, claiming the power of God. I didn't know what to say to her about the situation because she was so far away from hearing the truth. Her assumptions had to be that either she was Godlike, or she was in control of God, which was all too childish for me to fathom coming from a grown woman. I was completely thrown, but I knew it was significant to observe this situation for my own growth.

I tried to figure out what would make a person think in these terms and not be horrified with herself, or how she could think she had so much more power than she actually did. I didn't understand it then, but I now understand the wishy-washiness of Gray spirits, and she is one. I also had not understood the confusion that religion causes when people don't try and think things through rather than operate by rote madness, and when they don't really understand the nature of God. It is also a byproduct of thinking that good and evil are the point of this life—a misnomer many major religions teach. If you consider yourself good, it could make sense that God might destroy evil for you. This misguided thinking only applies if you don't understand God and are content to think like a child about these issues.

Of course if you buy into most of the religions, you are not well equipped to independently see God. Most religious doctrines prevent such independent thought and feed us whatever interpretations are appropriate for control. My friend was the unfortunate product of this in a way, because even though she was on a journey to understand God, she had not worked through enough of it to get her ego and her faulty teaching out of the way. I'm happy to report that she is beyond saying anything like that today, though I'm unsure how she processed the information. Apparently though, she has felt or thought her way through the obviously negative part of her stance about what had happened with her neighbor. Either that, or she just got wise enough to be quiet in these situations—which is still growth for a Gray.

The general rule for religion seems to be this: If the religious teachings advise you to hurt someone, or wage war, exclude anyone, or move in a direction that does not promote peace, the teaching is not from God or emulating the spirit of God, but is a manmade set of rules, pretending to be from God. The original intent of that religion and God's messages may have been given to a pure heart who did not interpret according to their own needs and desires. That person may have had the ability to hear or feel God strongly in the beginning, but somewhere along the line, somebody else put in their two cents worth and changed God's intent. Therefore, books explaining religious themes and doctrines that have been handed down and changed over years are not that reliable. Books written by too many people explaining the same set of rules are not reliable because you don't know who could actually hear, or truly feel God and who couldn't. There are too many interpretations along the way, made by too many other folks. Don't get me started talking about Paul in the Bible!

Getting back to my friend, another thing that is significant about this example is to know how to identify spiritual delineations. Generally speaking, a Light spirit would most likely not say anything like my friend's statement. Even if a Light spirit were angry enough to think it, they would know such a thing should not be said and would work hard to get this concept out of its thoughts. Neither would a Dark spirit likely make this comment because it lives with so many struggles with darkness that it knows how crazy true darkness sounds and it would not expose itself like this if it is working on spiritual growth. A Dark spirit might be inclined to make such a statement if it is not doing any real spiritual work, but even then, it may have done enough to know that people react to it like it is not well, and still might avoid the behavior. The reasoning is different, but the result might be the same. Generally a Dark spirit will keep its mouth shut. For the most part, a Gray spirit, in their childlike self-involvement, would actually open its mouth to say something this absurd. In some ways, the Gray spirit has the most difficult learning pattern because it misses so much learning as it is so engrossed in all-consuming self-involvement. Subsequently the Gray spirit does not listen well to what goes on around it and often does not notice how crazy or irrational it sounds.

Another one of God's intended tasks for us to understand is this: Often, religion gets in the way of spiritual enlightenment because there are so many misguided rules inherent in most religions that just keep us confused. These myriad rules can preclude us from doing the work we came here to do: connect and grow to be our best, so God can find the next God. We are probably supposed to be exposed to most religions, but we are also probably supposed to grow past it and let it go I think. It may be a stepping stone to addressing morality, but as we mature, we need to understand when it is no longer useful and only handicaps higher levels of thinking. It is our job then, to let it go, and work harder toward direct communication with our Creator. Religion may well be the day care center of spiritual development, but that's all. We become retarded when we try and hold on to it for a lifetime, because generally, it doesn't work. I wouldn't think that religion is effective after a few lifetimes, maybe between 25 and 50. Then it serves to stifle growth.

There are rare cases when a religious leader learns this concept also. At that point, this leader manipulates the language of the doctrine that is familiar to the followers, and twists it around a little to be more useful for helping us reach our best selves. These enlightened leaders are sometimes able to do a lot of good in the world, and they usually have thinking followers. When they speak, you rarely hear them fall into the exclusion and power trips. Their conversations are about what we need to do to stay close to God and how we need to function to be our true best selves and serve others. These people are amazing, but because they are so close to the doctrine themselves, they tend to get a concept or two a little confused sometimes. It's like a prisoner learning law from books. That prisoner still has to go to a courtroom and argue before they get the full meaning of being a lawyer, if they plan to be a litigator. The same is true with religion. If a person constantly feeds themselves the nonsensical religious doctrine of some religions, every once in a while they will believe it. These individuals have to free themselves completely not to incorporate it. However, they may very well have a lesson plan that includes service in a large way, and so they need a large following to accomplish their assigned tasks. That's between that person and God.

Generally speaking though, we just can't keep so much distance between us and God and expect to get the full picture. And we cannot go against His obvious rules and make our own that are clearly in conflict with, uh . . .uh . . . according to the books of your religion, God's own rules. You cannot say "thou shalt not kill" in one breath, and "hunt him down and kill the terrorists", in the next breath and really think you have this picture. Madness, sheer madness.

It isn't just Christians, Moslems, or Jews either, it comes in so many mad forms that it amazes me how disconnected, religious folks can be from God. I went to an Eckankar meeting, which is a light journey and believes that we are in school. The founder of this movement, Harold Kemp, might have well gotten some direct messages from God. His thinking is so clear in the literature he's written, and some of it is very much like the messages I have heard directly. In his books, Kemp refers to earth as a warring planet, but that we should strive to live on the Soul Plane with love as our concentration if we are to release the need to be at war. At the conclusion of the meeting I attended, after much sharing and love and light, and exchange of intelligent ideas, the woman who was conducting the local meeting said, in this very peaceful and loving environment, "So let us pray to support our troops in Iraq, so that they might win." I looked around, and nobody even flinched, but they might have just been cool.

I almost fell out of my chair!

She didn't say anything like "let's support all the people fighting this war, in hopes that they will find their way toward peace", or "may we pray that this war ends", or even "may we pray for the safety of our troops so that they may return to their families and loved ones" which might be one sided, but at least not supporting violence. She said "so that they might win." I think she missed the point of all that light, and overrode God's messages to her, Kemp's teachings and destroyed the efforts of the rest of the group that day. Must have whizzed right by her head!

I think that religion feeds into the "mob mentality" that takes over so much of American life (and possibly other cultures as well). This is my primary reason for saying that religion does not generally work. Even well-meaning folks get crazed, or forget their ability to process information independently when in groups. After that afore mentioned meeting, there were discussions about committees not doing certain things, and competition in the group, and blah, blah, blah. They missed the overriding point of the light acceptance for my taste.

This is the reason I believe that we have a massive, personal responsibility to make our life goal to connect directly to God. This can be accomplished with no mediators. We can not always discern what spiritual delineation any spiritual mediator is: a Dark, a Gray or a Light. That person may have their own religious hang-ups and their view of God may be faulty. Part of the reason I was hesitant to write this book is that, heaven forbid, the people who read this book might want to form a "group" with me as a guide. I know I'm not qualified to run a group, and I don't think this is the way God would have this proceed. I do; however, think we are supposed to share and learn information from each other. But the bottom line is we come here many times alone; and we leave here many times alone. If we get it right, only one of us will go make a new universe and start all over again.

It is my job to impart what I know, learn as much as I can, connect to others through God for the strongest and surest and least confused connection possible. I surely don't want to be confused, and I don't want to confuse anyone else. It is everyone's job to seek clarity, and God is clarity. Direct contact is our job, and frankly our only salvation as far as I am concerned. Then, we are better equipped to connect to others with the clarity of God. But a bunch of confused folks trying to explain God in the absence of God just won't work! Mob mentality will rule, and it doesn't rule well.

Religion can be a tool of the mob. However, in rare cases, (and they are far too rare), it can also be a tool of massive good if the real principles of God are actually followed with zeal. Now sometimes these leaders get it right and do incredible things because of their collective efforts. In these rare instances, religion is used correctly, to feed children, to help others get housing, for real mental and emotional support – not that with the threat of exclusion behind it, but with all the other things that are truly following in the directives of God. Generally, the folks doing the most good in these areas don't talk about "exclusion" of God's children.

I have never heard one evangelist with a large operation to feed, clothe, or house any people in other parts of the world say that they will not enter the Kingdom of God because they don't except Jesus Christ as their savior. These enlightened folks focus on the good and not on exclusion. I suspect that they have actually figured out how ridiculous it is to think that half the world's population is going to hell because they don't believe the same thing that they do. One can not work so closely in the work of God and remain ignorant, I hope. These savvy religious leaders just don't talk about it, because they have watched the mob turn against others who do. This partially explains why it has taken so long for me to step all the way out of this closet. America pretends to be about free thought . . . not hardly, generally speaking.

In conclusion, religion can work if it does not exclude or ostracize, does not hurt, does not condemn, and works for the good of all people. Those are God's principles in relation to group activity. Anything in opposition is man made, no matter what anyone may espouse as the source of their information. Often, the folks making those claims just haven't thought this concept through, or they haven't actually taken the time to hear God, and just keep filtering through a misguided intermediary. But bear in mind that they, like you and I, can change and grow. That is our job, and if they are working at it, they may well understand this part too in time. If they are thinking in terms of exclusion, wielding power, and hurting folks, I can almost guarantee they will have a very long time, and many more lifetimes to figure it out.

CHAPTER TWENTY FOUR
JUDGMENT VERSUS CONDEMNATION

There is a lot of talk today about how we should be careful not to pass judgment. People who embrace this way of new age thinking seem to think that it is a battle cry for enlightenment. I contend that they are confusing judgment with condemnation. If this new non-judgmental thinking is what people think is true, I'm afraid they may find themselves (as the old folks say) leaning on a broke stick, if they think this is a system of interaction with fellow human spirits that will endure during life's operations. We'd better make some judgments, but we should never condemn. It is not our right. Even God does not condemn, though he does have some special attitude adjusters for us, no doubt!

First of all, I find most people don't use the word judgment correctly. I will use my son as an example of people's misuse of the term judgment. For most of his life (though he is working his way out of it finally), my son is very, very stubborn, and learns very little, very slowly spiritually because of this resistance. This resistant makes his lessons quite hard because he really does believe that he is supposed to do what he wants, when he wants, despite all evidence to the contrary.

A couple of years ago, he was doing particularly foolish things out of stubbornness because he just didn't want to do it any other way because it would have meant work. Pisces seem to have particularly heavy lessons in laziness, moving only at their own pace despite all evidence that it is not working, and stubbornness, as do Diamonds in the Love Cards System, and he is both. He was heavily caught up in the nonsensical repetitive behavior syndrome, and yet he was confused as to why the same negative results kept occurring. When he said he wanted to discuss his behavior, I chronologically recounted the situations that had occurred, and the choices he made each time, despite the obvious, despite readings I received from God and ancestors on his behalf, which he asked for, despite the fact that even by his own assessment time after time, his decisions contained elements that had not worked before. At the end of my 10 minute recount, he said quite calmly, "I don't appreciate you judging me like this."

I had to fight not to react to his feigned attack, designed by his resistance. That is one of my major tasks to work through – not reacting or becoming annoyed when I see people's obvious manipulations. Most of these attempts are so transparent that it doesn't make sense that they think I, or anyone else, can't see through them. On that day, (and probably because I adore the ground the man walks on), I was calm and said "Where did judgment come into play? Didn't you do all of those things? I did not have to extrapolate or evaluate or draw any conclusions about your behavior, did I?" You could see the "Oh good grief" look on his face. At that point, the real conversation actually began, with his resistant nonsense falling by the wayside.

My point is this: People play so many games in order not to progress, because we are children in this journey toward being the next God. I have yet to fully understand why God started us out at such a low level in that first incarnation, as opposed to starting us out at the Gandhi, or Buddha place of enlightenment, but She did. I've been told that the reason is because of the complexities of the lessons we must learn, and how not one bit of it can be given to us because we would not understand it as fully. We must work for and earn the knowledge so that we know all things, all experiences in order to be the best new universe leader.

Having said that, we had better be able to judge and discern what is real and what is not, or we won't make it through this maze of difficulties and games and expected ultimate growth each lifetime. People usually don't know the actual meaning of the word judgment anyway. They misinterpret it to mean that somehow I (or whoever is speaking) am taking something away from them by stating what I see, which most of the time is obvious. They often also confuse criticism or even recounting facts with judgment if they are into the game playing activities associated with resistant learning. This is generally a tactic to make the person they are dealing with shrink and back off. That only works on people who are not seeking clarity. I have never seen it work on people who mean to move forward, only the ones who are resistant to change and intend to remain the same. The rest of us should and usually will forge on undaunted by such manipulations.

When I speak of judgment, I am using the meaning more in line with Webster's definition, *"the ability to come to an opinion of things;*

power of comparing and deciding; understanding; good sense." All the other meanings have to do with legal affairs, or God's judgment. Since I am neither a judge in a court, nor God, those meanings cannot apply to me or this discussion. These definitions also cannot apply to my son's protest. If I am only recounting facts as they happened, despite the fact that people in the "I don't want to hear this" mode would like for it to be different, there is no judgment on my part either. In operation and practical application this means I, and often you – the person grappling with the issue -- have observed this behavior in the past, and it is being exhibited today. This observation suggests an obvious pattern, which apparently, you are dealing with the consequences of same right now.

If we do not operate with discernment by paying attention to these behaviors and making judgments when dealing with other members of our Study Group, we will fall into our own repeated dysfunctional behavior, based upon participation with their nonsensical repeated behavior. Therefore, judgment is always necessary in order to know when to stop participation, and to discern what is real and what patterns they need to break, preferably without wasting our time. Judgment helps us understand when behavior is a real concern as opposed to when it is just locked in repetitive patterns.

However if you understand God, and what we are here to do, judgment never becomes condemnation. Judgment, or actually exercising judgment, acknowledges a person's present limitations and placement in the world and their own growth so that we can best operate with them and not damage ourselves. Condemnation, which is the assessment that they can never change for all time, oversteps self protection and self propelled growth. It assumes that we can determine what another spirit is capable of, or rather not capable of. We have then elevated ourselves to God's domain.

By virtue of the fact that we came here to grow, one would hope that at least on some days during each lifetime, we actually do that. Therefore, whatever I see today is what is going on today. But tomorrow, God may have helped that person have an entirely new perspective. Thus, each day I make sure spiritually and mentally I give every person a clean slate in my heart. I will assume that during the night, new lessons took hold, no matter how hard they are and no matter how long the person I am observing and interacting with has lived those lessons, or how many times I have seen them do the same thing over and over again. I will pay attention, and use sound judgment when dealing with them since I know what I have seen in the past, but as of today, I will not expect that same negative behavior unless, and not until, they act upon it or act it out. That way, I maintain my best spiritual self--which is always the goal. Otherwise, I do condemn the person to live down to my expectations, and that is certainly not to my spiritual benefit and growth.

Even God does not condemn. To assign such behavior to Him is a religious tool to control people. But condemnation, in this case using the Webster definition "to declare incurable", is never appropriate for human spirits looking to grow. We are too uninformed and too powerless to determine that to be true. Only God would have the power to determine that, and even She says She cannot, as a spirit may take many lifetimes to change. There is always hope people will change, and we all have the ability to do so. This is one of the reasons the concept of heaven and hell are so important to understand.

CHAPTER TWENTY FIVE
HEAVEN AND HELL

I suppose that in order to make any sense of this subject, I have to begin with what I know happens when we die. It is best for me to give examples of my experiences with other people's death. I've already written about Jeff and PD, but let me try and explain about people I've known who are close to me who have passed on.

In my first clear experience with death after getting a better understanding of these abilities, but before full control, I was given about three week's notice that my mother was going to die. She'd had a stroke and was mostly bedridden and in a wheelchair, and could not talk as a result. But I could still send her light and communicate with her in a form of astral projection, as she lived with my sister in another city. Basically I could look down upon her while she was lying in the bed and talk to her, and she would respond – subconscious to subconscious, similar to, but stronger than what we had done when I was a kid and she had exacerbations.

Three weeks before her death, I noticed that there were clouds between us which obstructed my vision of her in the bed. By the end of that week, there was a blanket of white cloudlike or cotton-like substance between us, and I could no longer see her. At the beginning of the second week, she began communicating to me through the clouds, where there had been no communication the week before. She was very calm and simply said that she was happy, and life had been wonderful. She was tired and ready to go, and she wanted me to help my sister let her go. This went on for several visits over the next two weeks.

It is important to include that about six months before, she had snatched out her feeding tube, wouldn't eat or let them put it back in for a few days, and was fading, having tried to leave before. My sister, who is usually very cool, jumped up on the bed, straddled my mother and grabbed her by the shoulders and shook her, shouting "You will not be leaving here on my watch, so just stop it!" She frightened the nurse, who called me later. My mother stopped fighting them and allowed them to put the tube back in. She sent me a psychic message that I needed to "help this poor crazed girl and help her deal with the guilt." I tried, but it was hard. My sister blamed herself for not finding my mother sooner, as she had the stroke in the middle of the night, and my sister assumed she was just sleeping late. She didn't find my mother until later that morning on the floor with a massive stroke.

I tried to prepare my sister, and told her I could no longer reach mother. She was calmer, I supposed, because even she recognized how nuts she was making herself, along with the rest of us, and prepared herself as she knew in her heart that mother had been winding down for months. Unfortunately, winding down and turning herself off were two different things in my sister's eyes, but she adjusted. One morning at 6:30 a.m., my mother smiled at her nurse and took her last breath. She was unavailable to me for quite some time afterward because I didn't have full control of my communications during this period. It would be almost four years before I could speak to her as a continued spirit, when I gained better control of the skill.

I had two friends depart before I could initiate conversations fully. At the time of their deaths, I had a fleeting feeling that they said goodbye. I was able to communicate with both of them after about a year. By then I had asked enough questions to know there is a resting period with spirits after they pass on, the length of which is dependent upon how difficult a time they had on this side before they left. I also understood from asking questions that at the moment of death, a spirit has knowledge of everything they have been involved with, and everyone they have been involved with, like a review and preview of sorts--a short period of knowing all. I suppose this is where the saying "my life flashed before my eyes" came from. During that time, they may stop by and say goodbye to those who can hear, but it is fleeting and quick as they head to their resting place. After they rest for a few months, they awake and begin the planning and work for the rest of their school assignments. That planning can happen only with God, or can happen with their Study Group of continued spirits.

After I was fully audient, the next person to leave was my sister. She had not communicated with the family much in the last few months, and was in hospice when my nephew called to say that I should come see her. I had gotten reports of her worsening condition from my mother who had continued on four years prior, so I knew of my sister's condition. She lived for about a month past that call, and I saw her often during that time period, though she slept a lot. On the night that she died, I had not been able to get over to see her all day long due to work. I intended to go early the next morning and spend most of the day with her. At 9:15 p.m., I was told, by God, to go to the hospice facility immediately, as my nephew would need me. I walked in the door exactly two minutes after she had passed at 10:02 p.m. that night. Of course, her son was quite upset.

I was told in that brief time that she was leaving, meaning within the first ten minutes after her death, while holding my nephew, she determined that she could have done better in this particular lifetime regarding reaching her best spiritual self. So, she set a goal to "wake up" very soon. She contacted me about four months later, the shortest resting period I have been able to identify yet from spirits I have known personally. She was gung ho about returning for the first year, but that enthusiasm has dwindled over time. The departed know how hard it is on this side, and in her case, she eventually did not really want to get back into this race so quickly after all. I can't blame her one bit.

In my father's case, things were a bit different. I had had enough conversations with him about what was happening to me for him to think I was losing my mind like my mother, but he decided that there was no other real evidence of that. However, he was cautiously in a state of suspicion about me for at least four years before he died. I pushed him on the issue because I wanted him to understand that my mother had not been crazy, but did possess a gift and ability she never fully developed because she believed she was crazy. None of this meant anything to him until about six months before he died.

If you will remember, I said that he was not in the pain he should have been in because of the prayers. However he began to ask me questions about my opinions of heaven and hell. That was very unusual, since he had pretty much discounted my opinions about spiritual issues. He was staunch Christian. About four months before his death, I was told to tell him that my sister would meet him on the other side. I didn't have the nerve at the time, but I was able to try and give him my opinion, based upon what I had been told, of what he could expect. At about three months, he began to see angels, a man, woman and a dog that were always walking beside him on a road. He could never fully see their faces as they always walked just slightly ahead of him. This was quite interesting since he did not like dogs. I asked God what he was seeing, and was told that they were distant cousins he had known when he was young. I told him the soft version of this, but he did not recognize them, but was calm and said that might make sense. I was amazed at how different the conversations were, in contrast to the years before.

As time moved on, he talked more about angels and situations he thought might be the after death scenarios. His new version of everything, including afterlife, was far softer than it had been all my life. I didn't get the three week warning like I did with my mother, and he had been at death's door so long, with sheer will had keeping him alive, that I was spiritually in a "I'm just here, waiting to see what I'm supposed to do next" mode. Then one day, I was told that he had a week to live but no continued spirits of God, had been giving me dates anymore for months, since all had been wrong before. Somehow I thought the message was a possibility that my father would just override, as he had done so many times before during the prior year.

Two of my sisters were present for his last moments. Because none of the things had happened in the manner that they did with my mother, I still didn't quite believe it until that morning when I asked God, and She said that this would be my father's last day. I panicked. I couldn't get to his city in time. I did not want to be there at his death because of the difficulty of being near people who passed over at that time, but I felt I should be there. I fully expected to be better warned I suppose, and thought that I could contact him subconsciously, as I had done for the four or five months before we reached that point. When I tried, I was told that he was too busy preparing to leave to speak with me. Guilt overwhelmed me. I called my sisters, and one of them told me that they didn't feel he had more than an hour left. She said she didn't know what was keeping him at that point. I asked to speak to him. She put the phone to his ear, and I said that I loved him and that my other sister would meet him on the other side. I told him he had been an excellent father, and I would be able to speak with him in a few months and to rest well. I apologized for not being there, but told him that I would always be reachable whenever he awoke. Ten minutes later, my sister called back and said he had passed on. While she was on the phone, I heard my father speak to me and say, "I'm okay honey, just fine. I love you." And then he was gone.

I learned a lot that day. First, I learned that if you get cocky, and have the nerve to think you know how something is going to go, God will allow you to learn differently, without warning. I also learned that each person's death, though it is the same in the scheme of things, can be a little different in actual action. I thought I had a handle on the rate of speed that his passing would take, and what form of communication I might have with him, based upon my experience with my mother. Wrong. It took him about six months to awaken and contact me. We talk now, but he is giving me room for the issues we are now able to work out that we couldn't work out while he was on this side.

These have been my most personal experiences with people passing over.

The primary question that most people grapple with: the existence of life after death has really been answered many times over in this book. This is my interpretation of all the information and readings that have come to me over the past few years. So the next question is, where do we go in between the school sessions? Where do we take our summer vacations, if you will?

The common Christian belief dictates that we go to the afterlife, and generally speaking, stay there for all eternity. This scenario isn't in synch with what I've been told. We do have to go somewhere in between. From what I understand, it is all in another dimension. It is all easily accessible to some degree, but quite distinct and inaccessible to another. It is not really far up in the clouds, but not too far from us in a way, and then not near us at all in other words. We can reach and communicate with anyone who has decided that they will speak to us in a blink of an eye. And the folk/spirits who have continued on are having a great time exploring and learning, and less often than not, they are not thinking about us, unless we need them. They are learning and growing and putting together their next lesson plan and getting it approved by God.

Additionally, those spirits who are in this place which seems quite heaven like, are often all around us, arriving at the call of our thoughts about them. Once they have completed their transition period, we can call them to us in essence, not in the holographic form, but the actual spirits, or they can visit when they want. Those spirits are about the size of the head of a thumbtack to a dime, which makes sense when you consider that God is the size of a Volkswagen really. They do what they want, and what they need to complete. They are concerned with folks from all the generations of families they had, on all planets, during their incarnations--not just the one in which they were related to us.

Within this same realm, there are several other areas in which other spirits reside. They are often separated from the families and may be in isolation according to what they learned, or failed to learn, while here, or wherever else they were – meaning other planets. As I said, there always is some truth to religion, from what I've been told, although often it is embellished. It is best for me to give the examples I know of.

My grandmother spent most of her life fully competent and in charge. After the death of her husband, she raised six children alone and was a fully self-sufficient businesswoman. At age 77, she forgot to keep the insurance up on her house, and a fire burned her home down to the ground. Her house had been her most prized and important possession and had provided her livelihood. She was devastated.

Her children began to formulate a plan to rebuild the house. However, all were fairly modest wage earners and had children in college, so it was taking time. My grandmother was not too displaced, as she lived with her daughter about a block away, but it may have worked against her to see her destroyed house every day. She was not really hurt during the fire except for a gash on her leg. This occurred when a young man dragged her out of the house because she did not want to leave her burning home. She was that attached, and her house meant too much. Of course, spiritually speaking, this is pride in the extreme, and this test was probably something she was to work through and not give in to. She did not seem to understand this lesson.

A couple of months into the process of her children trying to figure out how to come up with enough money to rebuild the house, my grandmother decided enough was enough. She announced to my aunt she would not be a burden to her children. She then called all of her kids, told them that she loved them, that they were wonderful children, but that she had had enough. She wasn't wild about staying around much longer and so she wasn't putting them through any more grief.

She said that they should get on with their lives and stop worrying about a foolish old woman too feeble to remember a simple thing like insurance. They protested, and reassured her of their love, but thought nothing of her speech since they planned to continue the business of finding the money for the house.

The following day, she began to have heart palpitations. My aunt took her to the hospital where they kept her for observation because of her age. By the next day she was no longer speaking, though not in a coma, and by the third day her heart stopped. The doctors had no clue as to the medical explanation. There was nothing wrong with her, though my sister reminded me later that she was showing early signs of diabetes. She just turned herself off with her incredible will. Of course this is my mother's mother, and the similarities of will appeared to be genetic. My grandmother simply willed herself to die.

I, of course, had many questions about this once I could talk to continued spirits, she being one of them, I thought. This is what I learned: I cannot speak with my grandmother because she is in a place that is inaccessible to me. It is also inaccessible to all of her relatives on the other side as well. It is somewhat of an isolation chamber, cool, and with no one else around. It is the "dunce corner" of heaven, or the other side, if you will. It is not dark, it is just isolated, and there are no other spirits around. It is the think tank, not cramped, like a jail isolation chamber, plenty of room, but nobody else present. My theory is if we get self involved enough to kill ourselves, we get to be by ourselves and think about nothing else but ourselves for quite some time. In other words, if we choose to be self involved enough to give up the game, we get to do that a little longer than we might have wanted. I have been told that prayer also works, so I pray for her to be allowed to join her family. But, I don't do it often enough. It is quite odd that I don't seem to remember this as much as I should. It doesn't make sense, other than the possibility that somehow God is making sure that I don't pray regularly about this and is blocking it somehow because He means for her to stay over there for a while.

Prayer is Her system to join us together as spirits, and if I prayed more often, I would be altering her being there I suspect, like my father's pain, as we all alter many things through prayer. God seems to want us to learn the lesson, so He would make sure the prayers were answered in this case because by praying, I am exhibiting understanding of this system and thus growth. By the same token, She must not want my grandmother out of that situation yet because she needs time there to learn, and thus, rather than disappoint me, and make me question my faith, He just conveniently helps me forget. That's my theory, but when I ask this I get "what do you think?" That's the standard answer at this point in my life because I am told less, and expected to think through things with the knowledge I have acquired more often than not. This is my interpretation of willful passing, or suicide. Giving up appears to be worse than hurting other spirits in a way, and these folks are not so easily assisted by other spirits.

I just read about Kevin Carter this morning through an e-mail. That's typical when God means for you to understand something, or do something in particular. I wondered why it came into my world this morning, but now I understand. Carter, the South African photographer, won a Pulitzer Prize for a photo in 1994 of a small, starving Sudanese child who was crawling her way to the famine relief center, and was struggling and stopped. Carter caught the picture of the girl slumped on the ground with a vulture watching her to see if she was going to die, so it could eat her. It is a stark, horrible statement about a world that lets children starve when there is so much wealth for a few, and nothing for so many. It also speaks to the severe racism in this world and the apparent planned destruction of African citizens, including her small and helpless children. It shocked the world and Carter, after long years of working with a group of photographers from South Africa who were determined to expose the horror there called the Bang Bang Club, committed suicide within months after receiving the Pulitzer. One of the last lines in his suicide note read:

"I am haunted by the vivid memories of killings & corpses & anger & pain . . . of starving or wounded children, of trigger-happy madmen, often police, of killer executioners . . . " And then this: "I have gone to join Ken (another member and close friend in the Bang Bang Club) if I am that lucky."

When you see the photo of the child, it's easy to understand the sorrow in Carter's heart, but still, that does not justify suicide in God's eyes. Remember this is all part of whatever test God puts before us. If the starving child in the picture still had the courage to move forward and try to live, surely Carter could have the courage to do his job and witness that horror. To do less dishonors the child's incredible will and courage, and is pure evidence of absolute arrogance and total self involvement.

We have difficult tests because they are part of our entire package of development. Sometimes, as in my case I've been told, part of the reason that things are so tough in our lives is because we committed suicide in a past life. So this is a sort of stress test, quite literally. I have been told that I committed suicide twice before. As my girlfriend said once to me, "So is God trying to make sure that you do it again?" That's sort of correct. She is really trying to make sure that I don't. I've been told this is part of the reason I became clairaudient, so I could handle and know why this life is filled with constant aggravation and so many disappointments. With that combination of information, I might not go the suicide route. As I said, God is a chemist, and this, thus far feels right. I believe now that no matter what I am faced with, suicide is not an option because I have way too much information to make that tragic mistake again.

The concept of suicide is tricky. When you think about it, a person has to be pretty self-involved, in all but the most extreme cases such as sacrificing yourself for others to live or such, to consider suicide. One has to be in their most spoiled state of "woe is me." I had a discussion with someone this morning about the subject, and he was saying that if a person found themselves paralyzed from the neck down, he couldn't say that suicide was not right for them. I can agree this person most certainly might want to die, but that is not their real decision. That is the decision and the right of the teacher, God, because we don't know what is to be learned during the time of paralysis. We only need to consider the life of Christopher Reeve in order to know all is not determined by the ability to walk, spiritually speaking.

Whatever experiences we undergo God has some reason for our ultimate spiritual benefit. Within this teaching scenario, we just don't have the right to quit school--which is what suicide ultimately is. However, because God is a merciful and kind God, if we really can't handle something, I truly believe that if we have done everything in our power to accomplish the tasks that we feel we must according to His instructions, then we should ask, and I believe God will grant deliverance. That is only if we have done all that we should. Making the decision on our own is not following the lesson plan and only gets us in trouble.

When I reread this section, I realize it could sound smug if we believe that we alone chart our destiny, and if we believe that our relationship with God is about good and bad. As I have said so many times in this book, from what I know, it is not. We are not rewarded and punished, not really. If something happens to us, either we caused it by not paying attention to the lesson in this life or a past one, or it is in part, the lesson, for whatever reason, perhaps to set us up for a future lesson, and we must work through it and have faith in its appropriateness for us.

Souls who committed suicides are in one place, and there is the place where PD was with her son. This location seems to be for spirits who are malicious and mean harm. They are together, but they are not with too many other folks, as far as I can tell. They just aren't allowed to intermingle and do many things that are pleasant. They are more living devoid of enrichment than in isolation like the suicide folks. These spirits don't have much they can do without seeing other equally errant spirits, and that is no fun. They have not given up their ways either so they are not allowed to enjoy much, but they can still carry out mischief, and are still learning from the other side. Still, apparently, they can be affected by this side, and by love. Love isn't enough for the suicide people. They are in a serious Time-Out, "dunce corner" kind of action going on there. The moderately errant spirits who act out of pain and suffering can still have contact with our world, but not the other side of their world.

There is another group. They would be in the closest thing to what we generally define as hell, but bear in mind, this is all God's territory. There is really no Satan, or Devil. God runs everything. We generate all negative energy, and God responds according to our actions. In discussing this other group, I can only provide an example of the only person I know personally who is there.

Earlier in this book I discussed a spirit who was only 8 lives old? In this life, she was the mother of someone I knew, and had pretty much sold her child into an incestuous relationship with her husband, because she was too lazy to work a full time job. She was a horror of a human being who was selfish, self-involved and would do anything to get what she wanted. This included allowing her husband to molest the daughter he had the most interest in from age 3 to 16. When her daughter finally stood up for herself, this woman did everything to destroy her. She threw the daughter out of the house, claimed she was trying to steal her husband and an array of atrocities up until her daughter's death at age 45, because of a disease, and in part because of a broken heart. Even then, the mother denied the truth and wouldn't admit she knew about the incest, even though the stepfather had admitted to it. Additionally, at every turn in the young woman's life, the mother did everything to make her feel evil and dirty, even telling her that she had to go and tell her first boyfriend what a "slut" she was. The daughter complied because she was so damaged and brainwashed she believed she was worthless.

This was a supposed religious woman. She stopped the drinking, cussing and smoking she did in her younger years, as well as the whoring around that she did before she got married to her molesting husband. This woman claimed to recognize evil, and she prayed every day to rid her daughter of this demon and tried to get her to stop "lying" (as she called it) about the molestation. This was her mantra. This woman has been my spiritual test as well, as she is the only human that I have had to truly struggle not to hate. I think I won my battle, but only just before she died. Yet before her own death, after years of making her daughter's life horrific, she did finally confess to a relative that she knew about the molestation, presumably, because she was trying to clear her conscience before meeting her maker. She wanted to go home to Jesus, having confessed her sins. Well, her trick didn't work.

She died of cancer of the throat (appropriate for such a liar it seems) and unable to speak for a while I was told, about five years after her daughter. She is in a different place than anyone else I know of who is a continued spirit. She is not allowed contact with anyone in this life or the next. She is in what has been described as nothingness, a complete void, not just isolation. It has been described as sort of suspension in total darkness, with no input, not even their own. That is the only discussion that anyone, including God, will have with me about her location. The continued spirits avoid discussion of the place, and most say they don't really know how to describe the little that they know. There is no telling when she will come out, or be sent back here, or somewhere else for her next lesson, but my gut feeling is not for a while, though I get no confirmations. This place is the closest to what has been described by some as hell, except I don't gather that there are other spirits there, and I don't sense that it is hot, just dark and empty. It is not a place under the control of anyone except God.

There are many places spirits go and they resemble what we have been led to believe, but there is a slant to it all. One of the best documentaries I have ever seen on the subject was titled "Hell", or "The Origins of Hell", produced by the History Channel, about the origin of what we consider to be hell today, and how we got that perception. The poem "Dante's Inferno" has much to do with the concept of hell we carry, but it has not always been the model for the popular concept of hell. I suspect that some of the writers of the Old Testament, which seems more accurate than the New Testament, really heard directly or had some other means of arriving at the information they used to deal with these concepts.

Understand too, that these thoughts reflect my present understanding of these holding places for continued spirits. I may know more later, but feel completely certain that if another place is needed, God will create it for Her students and may have done so already. I just don't know about it yet. Only God can determine where we will go for holding before our next return, or how long before we come back for additional class work.

CHAPTER TWENTY SIX

THE SHINING PUPIL OF OUR STUDY GROUP . . . RIGHT NOW

I only know three Dark spirits as friends or close acquaintances. One is out of my life now, primarily because of something he did that was very dark, though recently, he is making efforts to amend things; another is back in my life and making interesting and steady strides and progress; and the last is one of my closest friends. We'll call him Troop.

In certain areas of his life, Troop has been perhaps the most stubborn and difficult human being I have known, and yet could be very flexible in other areas. However, he had a seriously dark view of women and how he should treat them. He didn't have a deep respect for women and this attitude would come out every once in a while in his behavior toward the women he dated. First of all, he saw many women at a time, and he was never faithful to one woman and found no problem with that. Still, he was a draw for women because he could be very attentive and charming, and he never learned to treat women differently. To put it in his words, "I know every trick to get into a woman's pants, but I have no idea who they are." It was truly God's work that we ever became friends. Normally, I would have avoided a man like him as a friend, but he is loyal and supportive, even when he doesn't understand.

Over a period of about six years before I became fully clairaudient, we developed a deep friendship. I fussed at him about the way he thought of women, drinking, cigars, hanging out, and infidelity. Still our relationship grew because he has always had deep concern for me. Another thing was becoming apparent. He was deeply clairsentient, and picked up on quite a bit, quite accurately.

It is important to say here that our spirit delineation has nothing to do with our skills. You can be Clairaudient and Dark. One has nothing to do with the other except in God's plans. It is not a graduation to be Light, or to be able to hear. It is just your placement, and the thing that God wants you to work through, or work with. In fact a Dark spirit who comes and changes their delineation, in my opinion, has made much more progress than a Light spirit who comes here with less to work through, even if they maintain their Light status and don't partially regress. However, it may well be that the lessons are different as well, but at any rate, the concept of competition is not really applicable. This life we are living is only in competition with ourselves for the most part – to build upon past lessons, and complete all the tasks needed for us to be able to ultimately take over a new universe.

After, and while I went through the traumatic experience of becoming fully clairaudient, Troop was always there for me. But I always got the feeling that he thought I was just a little crazy. He only half listened to what I was saying, and whenever we would have deep, philosophical discussions about God and the experience I was going through, he would say something like, "Yeah, I guess that makes sense, If you buy into this whole thing, and I'm just not sure I do." So I would ask if he did not believe I was actually speaking to God. He would answer that I was certainly talking to someone, but he couldn't be sure it was God, but he had to admit that I knew things that I shouldn't.

One day, a couple of years into the process of me changing more thoroughly, I was told to tell him to read "The Spirits Book", by Allen Kardec, a centuries old journey into Clairaudience and other spiritual matters. I sent a copy to him, and told him what I had been told. He said sure, but I knew his reaction was half-hearted. As instructed, each week I asked if he had read the book, and he said that he had not. This exchange went on for about two months. Then I was told to tell him that it was no longer a request from Eva, but from God. Troop said, "Uh huh," and moved quickly to the next subject. About three weeks later I was told to pick up the phone and call him and ask if he had read the book. I did, and he said yes, part of it. I was told to encourage him to finish it within a week. He replied, "Uh huh."

A week went by, and I guess God got tired of his nonsense, and told me to ask again. I called him and asked again. He said yes he had finished the book. I believed him and actually began to ask about parts of the book and how he felt about it. Mid sentence, I was told by God, while still on the phone to hang up, that he was lying. This was the first time, though not the last, that I had ever been in the middle of a fight between someone and God. I asked "What? I'm sorry what did you say." Again, I was told to hang the phone up immediately, because he was lying. I told Troop what was happening, and that I had to get off the phone. He protested that he was not lying. I told him that I thought he better fix whatever was going on, but before I could finish the thought, I was commanded to hang up the phone immediately. I did, mid his protest, and as soon as I did, I was told that I could not speak to him again until I was given permission, and that I was not to ask for same. I would be told when that would be. I was dazed, but I don't mess around with direct orders anymore.

After two days, Troop called and left messages for me to call. I didn't. I didn't ask, and I didn't return his calls. My earlier case of hives ended all disobedience of that nature, period. I felt sorry for Troop for allowing himself to get into a fight with God, but I could do nothing to help him. I might have tried some different prayers, the begging kind, if I thought they might help. But I knew better. I prayed for him to gain enlightenment and understanding and to release his stubbornness. Troop's messages got downright pitiful, then arrogant and defiant, and finally funny. First he claimed he had read the book, and didn't know why he was being lied upon. Risky business for a non-lightening proof entity for my money! Still, he remained incredibly diligent in his nonsense. I still was not allowed to talk to him, and I didn't ask.

I prayed for a case of the hives for him, just so he could put things in perspective and not be so downright stubborn and silly. I was told that he had been incredibly lazy for many lifetimes, and that the hives, in combination with the Dark spirit, would not have the same effect on him that they did on me. They would make him more stubborn and he would have to be seriously hurt to get results and that was not God's aim. God only wanted him to stop the defiance which had no useful purpose. He had allowed himself to give God leverage—me!

This tact was extremely ridiculous for a person who needed, at that time, many anchors, of which I was an important part of his stabilization system. Why he would take a chance like that was beyond me, but as I said, we are not the brightest pupils on the block if we are here. At one point, God, laughing (which She does a lot at us) said that Troop thought he was in a struggle in which he was at war with God, as if She were any other person, and felt that my love for him would outweigh my obedience to God, and that I would pick up the phone and call him. Sadly, the thought of a fool who has never had hives that were on fire for twenty minutes! He was leaning on a broke stick. Remember, God has said that our free will is the only thing that keeps this game interesting enough for Him to stay awake basically. Troop gave Her a great show.

I was allowed to ask another friend to call him and tell him that I could not speak to him until he read the book, so leaving the sad phone calls made no sense, and for him to just read the blasted book, please! She did. Still, he did not read that book for a couple more weeks. The whole ordeal took about three months! What incredible stubbornness over reading a book. I was amazed.

Then one day, God said, as I was cooking dinner, "You may call Troop now. He has read the book, a little half-heartedly, and he skimmed a few sections, but I'll let that slide for the moment." I called him the next day, and we reconnected happily. I asked him what in the world was on his mind. He said he just refused to have somebody tell him what to do like that, but that he was tired of not talking to me, so he finally read the book, and by the way, it wasn't so bad.

God is merciful, and we are not bright.

I've asked Troop to tell me what he was thinking, as it might be helpful for the readers of this book.

Eva: When did you determine that my experience was different from the norm and what did you think?

Troop: The differences became important when the reading of the book came into play, because it was too real, and that was when the light switch went on. I could no longer determine that it was just your imagination that was leading the discussions. There was no doubt in my mind then of who you were talking to. That's when I started to get really annoyed with the whole spiritual issue and it was not comfortable then, even though in some ways it was exciting.

The reading about me reading "The Spirits Book" was me testing God, trying to make him play parlor games. I thought that either you were talking to someone else and you were crazy, or this was really God you were talking to. I had trouble conceiving that God would want to talk to me, or you for that matter. God doesn't talk to people like you and me. He only talks to people like Charleston Heston and Jeffrey Hunter, and you didn't look like none of those people.

Eva: So how did you think you could test this?

Troop: I just wasn't going to take any of it seriously. If you were crazy, you just thought you were talking to God, and I loved you but you were losing your mind. I wasn't getting caught up in that stuff. I had enough problems. So I thought that by not reading the book and yet telling you that I had, there would be no way that you would know and then it would eliminate all of this discussion and then you would just shut up and all this nonsense would go away. I was a little interested in the book, but I was resistant to reading it because I didn't really want to get involved in the spirit world. I don't really know why, but I think that being at a crossroad in my life, laziness and fear of having to change and be different from what I knew, and of "being with God", would not work because God would know me, but I didn't know God. I had a whole lot of trouble believing that God would want to talk to somebody like me? I was corrupt and sacrilegious as I have been in my life, and so I felt somehow that if I was being disobedient that somehow it would all go away. I figured He would just get tired and forget about me. I didn't say it was sane, but I thought if I can get away from everyone else who gets on my nerves, then I could get away from Him. (big laugh)

Eva: What was the big deal?

Troop: I didn't want to change and He was requiring me to change. I equate it to trying to go backward, and God flips you around so you end up moon walking, but still moving in a forward direction. No matter what I did, I was still being forced to move toward God.

Eva: When did you figure out that it wasn't me, but actually something else was happening?

Troop: It came to me the first time that He told you to hang up the phone on me because I lied about having read the book. I realized that it was certainly someone on the other side that you were talking to. I didn't want to believe that you could talk to someone on the other side, because when I was alone, I wanted to be alone, and didn't want to think that there was a whole group of folks around me paying attention to what I was doing. Anonymity was much better, and that wasn't reality. But then I had to think about all the little lessons I had been paying attention to all my life, and so it became confusing, because I knew, somewhere in myself that I was able to "know" things before they happened, and I tried to ignore that. This would mean that there was actually someone else talking to me and telling me things. Reading the book would be an acknowledgement of that, and I just didn't want to do that.

Eva: What made you finally read the book?

Troop: Fear of losing you, and having someone telling me that I couldn't talk to you, and God knew that, so I finally read that book. I just wasn't going to be forced to do something. Clearly, there are times that I have just not been that bright, and so I thought I could defy. It has only been after watching and participating in the miracles that I have been party to and that have surrounded your life that has made the difference. Accepting the existence of a living God takes some work when you have been resistant all your life.

Eva: Why?

Troop: Before, God was only somebody I had a conversation with about what I did in life at the pearly gates, and then I could cop a plea later about all I had done wrong and he would do whatever at that time. Avoidance was the operational method. I wasn't even sure what would happen and if copping a plea would work, I just wasn't going to think that hard about it, and I wasn't moving toward change.

Now I understand that talking to God is normal and not abnormal and that we all have the ability to talk to God. And what we don't know how to do is listen to God, and I'm the King of not listening, and I'm sure that He has put other people in my life who could show me other ways to approach this, but of course I wasn't listening to them. He would put spiritual people in my path that I had not listened to and ignored before knowing you. But you and I had a different kind of a relationship and we had bonded in other ways before we got to spiritual discussions, and then he kaboomed me by manipulating me through you, and then using you to make me listen. Then He also made sure I was hurt, (**Note:** Troop suffered a major back injury that left his foot partially paralyzed in 1997 – we met in 1995) which then made me pay attention to other things instead of basically ignoring them. The physical disability forced me into thinking about something other than myself, and I was forced to think outside of myself. But still He was not a living God, but was distant, until the book incident. Then He became most definitely, "The Boss."

Eva: Two years after that book incident, you stopped all spiritual work you had diligently done as a result of it, and got real stubborn, went back to drinking, smoking, undisciplined behavior, and basically whining. When you regressed again, what was driving you?

Troop: That was about responsibility for other people outside of myself, and I didn't want to be responsible to you and didn't want to participate in spiritual growth. I wanted to do what I wanted to when I wanted to, but nothing would work right because I went back into an altered state. Also I got very angry with God about my back injury because I didn't think He had to turn me into a cripple in order to accomplish the task of spiritual growth. But I doubt that I would have grown otherwise, because I would have continued to live a decadent lifestyle and not do anything to grow. I would have made the same money and been having a great time and would have done nothing new, because my only goals would have been to make money, and enjoy money. There would not have been any serious purpose outside of just getting things and seeing my children and grandchildren grow. But there would have been a huge void without actually knowing God. One of the most important exercises was when I went to the flea market to sell my work, and you told me that God said it would help me spiritually. I felt that all I needed was money, and how was spiritual help going to help me in the real world. How important it is to lead with something spiritual and how that makes you feel is so different when you do so. I was tired of being challenged all the time and I wanted to be lazy. I didn't want to do anything that was that much work. Laziness is my worst bad habit, and I still struggle with it daily, but I fight more to conquer it.

Just yesterday, I didn't want to go to the Dojo, so I went to go take some photos of a client. But I stopped just short of him to catch the subway where I wanted to take a photo of a man on the street, when I realized I had no video card in the camera, and so I couldn't do either thing – the client nor the man on the street. But I was close to the Mari Kari Dojo, and I realized that that was the real reason that God took me to that neighborhood. I was told to go to the Dojo in an earlier reading, and I had not done it, so now I was led there. Now I notice. I now know that God will help me stay on a spiritual path, but that He won't do everything for me. I'm understanding that now.

Eva: What is different now than before the book incident?

Troop: I'm learning how to love God now, instead of what I was doing before, which was ignore His existence. And I'm learning that from a reading you gave me earlier, when He said that I had done as much as I could do with my life with my own devices. Now that I have turned it over to Him, as much as I can at this growth level, and really I was not doing that good of a job on my own, and now that God is running more of it and I am more obedient, and it is going a lot better. Now I am starting to figure out what turning over really means. It doesn't mean that you are not pro-active, but you do what you can, and take it as far as you can, and then turn it over and allow God to do whatever He feels is right after that point. You have to do all you can and then decide that whatever God does after that is okay.

One of the things that has happened also, is the lack of fear I now feel. I wasn't accustomed to living with a lack of fear in my life. Now I don't think about being afraid and upset about things. I seldom get mad about things and now I look forward to being what I want to be and not what is blocking me. I just do the things I am supposed to regardless and I don't let anything stop me now because I feel that God is with me and that means it is okay. I am much more concerned with whether or not I am doing all I can to make myself proactive. I came to the conclusion that I have to grow up, and you do that by participating and putting things in order, and I have a lot to put in order, which challenges my laziness.

I neglected a lot of things because I was so lazy. So now I have to work really hard. People, places, things, work, they all must be in order now, and the result from me doing this work is that I feel younger, and in love with life, and I think I'm loving God more, which is new to me. I think I love everyone a lot more and I'm less angry. Now, at the end of the day, I'm not as angry because a lot of the things that have to do with anger are actually my own self-involvement. I'm confused about a lot of things, but only confused "scratch your head", but more often, not confused "bewildered." I try and keep an open mind. I'll at least ask myself why I might have a minor confrontation, whereas I never asked myself anything before. I do anger much less than I used to.

Eva: Anything else that's important?

Troop: I don't think I'm the poster child for the Study Group. I'm the example of how not to become spiritually aware. I'm actually the poster child of unnecessary resistance. Understand my example and don't take the charge. If I'm a poster child, its about how not to run away from a golden, written invitation from God for clarity, and love. Don't resist so hard, because I made a job out of resistance, which got me a serious lesson in learning that once I stopped resisting, my life drastically changed and now 20 year old dreams are coming true. I am actually associated with emotionally, mentally and spiritually the artistic things that I moved to New York to accomplish and do. The only serious flaws I have are the ones in my character and in my laziness and admitting it. Those are my serious challenges, not the challenges of life itself.
(**Note**: Troop was in another field of work that was physical, though he always wanted to be a photographer, but allowed himself to get sidetracked.)

Eva: How do you feel about your back injury now?

Troop: Every time I take a photograph, I owe it to my back injury, and that was due to my lack of care, and God allowing me to learn my lesson. I owe my new career to my so-called disability. I am pursuing and living my own dreams. This time next year, I feel I will be real surprised. I feel it every time I let the shutter loose. I had a shoot with a famous person yesterday, and I had a great time. Even when there is no pay, I like my work.

End of Troop's personal account.

There is more to Troop's story that is extremely significant. He is the only person I know who has graduated from one spiritual delineation to another. He is no longer a Dark spirit. He has moved to become a Gray spirit. I was told that this is very rare, but I saw the hard work over about a three year period. The manner in which he processes information, life, relationships, God, everything is totally different. And because he is a Dark moving toward Light, he does not seem to have quite as much of the wishy washiness that I see in many Grays. This was his reading on the day I was told that he had graduated. I asked him what was different about that day before I told him of the graduation. He said that he had made some decisions about life, and people, and that he had released something, and he just loved everyone all of a sudden, and was happy to be alive.

You would have to know how far this was from anything I had ever heard from him to fully appreciate the weight of his statements. He used to blame anybody, everybody and anything for his shortcomings, and he was clear that little was his fault and that God was conspiring against him, along with a few other folks. To hear the change was phenomenal! Here is the reading/message from God of that day:

12-24-05

God: Troop has acquired some protection in life. He has been granted a guardian angel named Edward, who will help him through some of the more difficult times in his life and his decisions that affect his growth and improvement from this point forward. He has earned the help, but he must understand that with it comes great responsibility. He is not allowed to just pass on most things that he has tried to before, meaning, that when he sees an injustice, he can no longer act as if it is not his issue, ever. When he sees injustices to women he can no longer act as if he has no clue about what is going on. He has worked hard, very hard to change his point of view about women, and so now, he has gone to a new level in his understanding, which is excellent. He has made more progress about women in this lifetime, than he has in the past 8. He will make a major breakthrough in this major lesson if he continues to do what he is doing and work hard. He must also work equally hard at getting his vices under control, or there will be consequences. He can no longer neglect his health and that means he needs to find and stick to a real exercise program. They have plenty of yoga tapes that he can do at home. He can also and must work harder at maintaining his health. He does not eat wisely, and he eats too much, and it is not healthy. He needs to do his own research and work on these areas like an adult. He has acted like a child regarding these areas and now it no longer fits his new level of spiritual maturity. He must get all of it in line. Edward will be watching him closely and in part, his job is to help Troop establish a more mature manner in which to see the world, not just as pertains to women, but as it pertains to himself.

Eva: Did you keep him from going home for the holidays?

God: Yes, he was not ready for what was awaiting him. He is too fresh in his changes and these kinds of situations will throw him off at this point. He will be ready in the summer to see his mother, but a lot of work is coming between now and then. He must do that work. He is about to embark upon a whole new level of learning that he has not imagined. It is time for him to rid himself of all of his childish fears, and childish indulgences. He has adult work to do, and he needs to do that work. He needs to pray and fast, cleanse his soul and body.

Eva: Is his guardian angel Edward, his father?

God: No, he is not. He was a much older man when he died in his last incarnation, in his 90's, and he did a lot for the world with his attitude. He was a generous man, who understood and liked women. Part of the reason he was chosen for Troop. He also was a generous hearted man who did more to help the world than his means might have suggested he would. He was active in the community and did a lot of work to better the world. He was not American, but Armenian.

End of reading.

I still think he is the poster child for spiritual growth, and I'm happy and honored to know him.

CHAPTER TWENTY SEVEN
STRANGE ENOUGH!

I suspect that for this first book, this has been enough. If you've stuck with me this far you must be a very open-minded person; a kindred spirit in the Study Group; or you thought it was too strange to leave . . . sort of like a train wreck or car accident. Whatever the reason, thank you for reading my coming-out endeavor. I feel certain that my journey will be enriched from writing this, and I hope that as time goes on, parts of this might seem more plausible, or at least not so far fetched to those who consider it so.

We are embarking upon a spiritual evolution/revolution, and I suspect that many things will seem commonplace in another 20 years. New paradigms are being developed and insisted upon. New language, new thinking and open mindedness are essential for our collective and individual growth. Doctrines that seek to control will likely become obsolete, so it is best that we learn to be self-governing, in conjunction with the highest ideals, and within, and surrounded by the most light.

May the light of God guide our endeavors, and may we move closer to His/Her/Its light with every action we take and every breath we breathe.

If you found this book useful, you can get more copies at:
http://www.lulu.com/content/604034 or ***www.spiritsetfree.com***
or *www.thenextgodbook.wordpress.com*

Also look for my short book **The Law of Attraction Can Kiss the Left Side of My Behind! (And That Ain't No SECRET) at *www.lulu.com/evaravenwood.***

I welcome your comments and questions. Please send them to **spiritsetfree@yahoo.com**.

Thank you, and may we all operate in brilliant light
and preparation for the new spiritual models!

EVA

BOOKCOVER DESIGN

Carl W. Nunn * Front Cover Photo
www.imagesbynunn.com imagesbynunn@yahoo.com

http://www.rangefindermag.com/repository/rf/articles/pdf/RF1008 Hunter Kolesnikova.pdf

A native of New York State, Nunn has spent many years in the film, photography and visual image industry. Carl W. Nunn began taking pictures as a teenager and later studied photography at the Center for the Media Arts. He spent more than a decade working in films. His film experience helped develop his unique frame of reference and respect for the placement and positioning of objects. "Nunn's work is captivating and inspiring" says Janifer Wilson, owner of Sisters Uptown Bookstore LLC in Harlem, New York.

Carl W. Nunn was born and raised in Syracuse, NY. At the age of twelve he began shooting photos and processing film with the help of a photography professor at Syracuse University. Mr. Nunn moved to New York City in the summer of 1986 to study photography at the Center for the Media Arts. He pursued a career in fashion photography, but soon found a stable job working in film. For ten years Carl worked as a key grip for major movie productions. Mr. Nunn's work as a grip – setting up scenes for cinematographers and directors – helped develop his unique frame of reference and respect for the placement and positioning of objects. Carl's training as a grip set the stage for his recent return to photography, with a focus on the new digital format.

Mr. Nunn's first exhibition "Where Harlem Meets the Sky" is the first of a series depicting Harlem's landmarks and buildings in the context of natural elements like the sky, the sun and the moon. Nunn was inspired to shoot sky views of Harlem because he desired to capture Harlem's natural beauty in a light that had never before been realized. Mr. Nunn currently lives and maintains a studio in Central Harlem.

W.A. Bridges * Eva's photos * Atlanta, GA

Hugh Marshall * Cover Design
www.myspace.com/airhue * e-mail - hughmarshall@bellsouth.com

Hugh A Marshall, a native From New York, is an aspiring artist in all types of mediums. He is an illustrator by trade and has many illustrations published in books. His most recent accomplishment is a children's book called "Sydney's Saddest Sunday".

Bill Alger * Cover Design
http://www.photoshopuser.com/members/portfolios/view/gallery/35825

RESOURCES

Understanding Chakras:

http://www.thirdeyehealth.com/chakras.html

http://www.astrologyweekly.com/astrology-articles/chakra-system-charts.php

http://www.rolandberard.com/Production/FR/Chakras.htm

http://www.eclecticenergies.com/chakras/open.php

http://www.scns.com/earthen/other/seanachaidh/chakras.html

SUGGESTED READING

If you don't get caught up in details, but stick with the gist of things, most religions, most philosophies and most humans, despite cultural differences, have more similarities than not. So I read a broad, cross-section of information and try and keep my opinions to myself while trying to learn. It is my belief that if we do not train ourselves to have tolerance for other people's faiths and differences in spiritual thinking, we are all going to lose our lives in senseless religious conflict. That's why we can't opt for the easy way out, because we have serious, adult work to do. These are in no particular order.

The Shift –
Owen Waters
What I learned After Medical School –
O.T. Bonnett, M.D.
Why Healing Happens -
O.T. Bonnett, M.D.
Reincarnation: The View From Eternity –
O.T. Bonnett, M.D. with Gregor Alan Satre

Man's Search for Ultimate Meaning –
Viktor E. Frankl
The Crisis of Our Age –
P.A. Sorokin
Money Talks; Power Talks – The New World Disorder – Samuel V. Duh
Empathy and the Practice of Medicine –
Edited by Spiro, Curnen, Peschel and James
Food of the Gods – The Search for the Original Tree of Knowledge – Terence McKenna
The Power of Healing –
Edited by Reader's Digest
The Crucible of Race –
Joel Williamson
Inside the Third World –
Paul Harrison
Beyond Freedom and Dignity –
B. F. Skinner
Beauty and the Priest –
Reverend Patrick McNamara
Is Jehovah An E.T.? –
Dorothy Leon
Worlds Beyond Death –
Dr. Grant H. Pealer, D.D.
Pathologies of Power – Health, Human Rights, and the New War on the Poor – Paul Farmer
Love Blocks – Breaking the Patterns that Undermine Relationships –
Mary E. Donovan & William Ryan, Ph.D.
Hebrew Myths: The Book of Genesis –
Robert Graves and Raphael Patai
Psyche & Symbol –
C. G. Jung
The Book of the Dead –
Introduction by E. A. Wallis Budge
Determinism and Freedom in the age of Modern Science – Edited by Sidney Hook

The Rainbow People of God – the making of a
peaceful revolution – Desmond Tutu
Flash of the Spirit –
Robert Farris Thompson
Divining The Future –
Sally Morningstar
The Politics of Religious Conflict – Church and
State in America – Richard E. Morgan
World Religions – from ancient history to the
present – Edited by Geoffrey Parrinder
Saintly Advice – A prayer for every problem
The Philip Lief Group, Inc.
A United Religions Koinonia –
Thomas A. Wright Sr.
Human Values and Abnormal Behavior –
Walter D. Nunokawa
Atlas of the World's Religions –
Edited by Ninian Smart
Awaken Healing Energy Through the Tao –
Mantak Chia
Contact The Other Side – seven methods for
afterlife communications – Konstantinos
Putting Emotional Intelligence to Work –
David Ryback
Hands of Light –
Barbara Brennan
Ordinary People as Monks and Mystics
Marsha Sinetar
The Secret Language of the Soul –
Jane Hope
The Sacred Hoop –
Paula Gunn Allen
Hope and Suffering –
Desmond Tutu
Good Life, Good Death – Tibetan Wisdom on
Reincarnation – Rimpoche Nawang Gehlek

Wisdom of the Mystic Masters –
Joseph J. Weed
Every Eye Beholds You -
Edited by Thomas J. Craughwell
The New Psycho-Cybernetics –
Maxwell Maltz, M.D.
The Transcendental Meditation Primer –
Patricia Drake Hemingway
Tales of Yoruba Gods and Heroes –
Harold Courlander
Where Are You Going? –
Swami Muktananda
Emerson – The Mind on Fire –
Robert D. Richardson, Jr.
Love Cards –
Robert Camp
How Good People Make Touch Choices –
Rushworth M. Kidder
The Holy Qur'an –
Edited by A. Yusuf Ali
Ifa Divination – Communication Between Gods and
Men in West Africa – William Bascom
Integral Spirituality –
Ken Wilber
The Road Less Traveled –
M. Scott Peck
People of the Lie –
M. Scott Peck
The Spirits Book –
Allan Kardek
The Medium's Book –
Allan Kardek
The Reach of the Mind –
J. B. Rhine

INTERESTING WEBSITES

www.damanhur.org

www.kenwilber.com

http://www.cpwr.org/

http://www.readersread.com/booklinks/bookpublishers/relig.htm

http://www.interfaith-presidio.org/links.html

http://www.wie.org/misc/about-wie.asp?ifr=util

http://www.worldfaiths.org/moreinfo.htm

http://interfaithalliance.org/home

http://www.worldinterfaithclergy.org/index.php?option=com_frontpage &Itemid=58

http://www.alextanous.org

http://www.sukyomahikari.org

http://www.worldpeaceemissaries.blogspot.com

ABOUT THE AUTHOR

Eva Ravenwood is a Clairaudient and Spiritual Mystic/Medium/Psychic with clients worldwide, and Author of the book ***The Next God*** and ***The Law of Attraction Can Kiss the Left Side of My Behind! (And That Ain't No SECRET!)***. She works with clients worldwide, and conducts seminars on defining and embracing spiritual similarities and differences in other people, thereby improving working and family communications for corporations, universities and associations.

She is also Host and Executive Producer of the internet radio blog series ***The Spiritual Envoy***, which can be heard in archive on the internet at ***http://www.blogtalkradio.com/thespiritualenvoy.*** Other parts of the series include ***The Spiritual Mom's Corner***, with Host Danah Hilden and ***The Spiritual Educator*** with Mike Seymour, both found at the same address. Please listen live on most Mondays at 6:30 pm, EST, or in archive at Blog Talk Radio or the Spirit Set Free! website.

Eva Ravenwood * P.O. Box 50473 * Atlanta, Georgia 30302
www.spiritsetfree.com

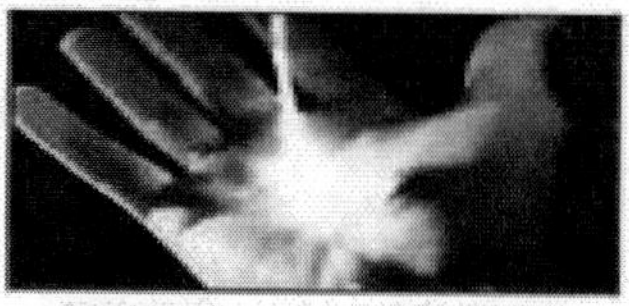

Spirit Set Free!

grab your spark of freedom!
www.spiritsetfree.com

SPIRIT SET FREE! INTERACTIVE WEB COMMUNITY

Over the years Eva has come to understand her clients and their needs better. Unable to keep up with the demand for readings, she is creating the interactive website Spirit Set Free, which will be up and running March 1, 2008, and can be found at ***http://www.spiritsetfree.com***..

Spirit Set Free is an online community managed by Eva Ravenwood. It was developed to offer options for spiritual thinkers to navigate our complex world using simple spiritual methods for communication without hidden dogmatic inferences. Eva has been a Clairaudient (one who hears clearly) professionally since 2001, and has been aware of her sensitivities since childhood, when she learned to communicate psychically with her mother (a medium who was misdiagnosed as schizophrenic) when she entered other states of awareness. This early training, along with doing soul level readings for hundreds of clients, built her understanding of the diversity of spiritual models under which human spirits fall. With that understanding she sought to connect the dots between religion, mysticism, continued spirits or the afterlife as some call it, and our practical spiritual operational methods that we use on a daily basis. From that has resulted the Spirit Set Free! community for spiritual cohesion and growth for all schools of thought and people of every religious persuasion who are willing to soften the lines for the greater good of us all.

Its purpose is to provide online classes, seminars and courses in spiritual development, discussion groups, forums, social networking, spiritual gifts and cards, and an array of services provided by other practitioners in one place, so that clients can find most of what is needed for spiritual health and wellbeing, all under the same virtual roof.

SPIRIT SET FREE
WORKSHOPS AND SEMINARS FOR
CORPORATIONS, UNIVERSITIES AND ASSOCIATIONS

The world is evolving, spiritually speaking, and the dogmatic systems that held for centuries, often no longer promote effective communication between diverse people. We need new leaders who approach belief systems with flexibility that better reflects the actual diversified population of our planet, With that understanding, progressive thinking and behavior must come in all facets of life, including, and actually especially spirituality, because what a soul believes, guides how she or he will govern their home life, businesses, children, community and thus the world.

Those in power have an especially weighty responsibility to be alert, spiritually even-handed, clear and inclusive thinking if we are to provide enough resources for our planet to survive. Should we fail to do this, the chasm between the haves and have nots will escalate into policies and decisions that will steal the value of our soul and remove us from all possibilities of achieving our spiritual greatness, which far outweighs our material prowess.

To that end, these seminars are designed to assist present and future leaders in developing their inner light, so they might spark the world brightly!

These hour long seminars are designed to provide ways to release dogma and find common operating systems with people possessing dissimilar spiritual foundations.

If you are interested in Eva coming to your establishment, contact her at
e-mail – **spiritsetfree@yahoo.com**
or call Eva at **404 – 671-7754**

THE HAZING PROJECT

If you or someone you know well hears voices, please read this article, and participate in the collection of data if you should so choose. Thanks.

THOSE VOICES YOU HEAR IN YOUR HEAD MIGHT BE "HAZING"
October 30, 2008

Hazing (my term) is the place where people who are developing their abilities as mediums just begin vibrating high enough to connect with the spirit world. Unfortunately, the first spirits that can be connected to are the ones who vibrate at the lowest frequency, and they are usually disruptive, negative, mischievous and annoying if not downright mean and hateful. They often seek to confuse a person and keep them running around in circles in their head. They will tell you to hurt yourself or others, or that you are nothing, or that people don't love you and actually hate you when you thought they loved you. Their only purpose is to be ugly to you. They are angry and confused, and want you to be the same.

For the sake of explanation, not necessarily completely accurate, think of a thermometer, and at the bottom is zero. Let's say that that is the average frequency of the internal vibrations or electrical measure of most people who do not hear voices. As mediumship develops, a person who can hear the first voices, the negative ones, might be at 10 vibration, and that negative communications pick-up (think of it as radio waves) may last till you get to about 30 as there are many different kinds within this range. Then after that you get to the benevolent spirits, usually in your ancestral line as they are easier to hear first, that might be from 31 to 45, and then spirit guides, from 46 to 55, and Angels, from 56 to 65, and other beings, all the way up to God at say 90 or so. Although it is important to note that I suspect that God and Angels can reach us, no matter what frequency we can achieve.

If you think of it this way, you are just moving up the scale. But you have to move, or you stay stuck in the lower vibratory communications and then are afraid, frustrated, angry (which lowers your vibrations) and all other manner of systems that don't help your cause of getting out of where you are. Usually, medication won't stop the voices either, so then you have an added issue of taking a chance and going off of them because they don't work for you, which is not good, or always being drugged and the effects of that on your body, and still hearing voices, and that is just not pleasant!

My mother stayed there most of her life. When the abilities began with me and the negative voices started, I knew her example was not one I wanted to follow, and researched and began many hours of prayer. I do mean many – sometimes 8 hours a day -- for a couple of years, but I learned a lot about raising vibrations, and enough to help some people like me and her find a shortcut to some of what I learned. Let me say at this point, I have never been diagnosed as having any mental illness because I don't, and hearing voices doesn't affect my life adversely after I got through hazing, which I will not lie to you, was a rough few years – but I fought accepting that I was ill because I heard voices, unlike my mother who accepted that diagnosis. Now nobody, as in unseen continued spirit folk, talks to me unless they ask permission, or unless I ask permission. I am loosely monitored by three psychologists, two of whom I now work with their clients because after years of watching me, they are developing different views of this.

If you elevate your vibrations, and that can happen through non-begging prayer, *(that means no help me Jesus, please just make it go away, help me, help me -- as that is a prayer of desperation -- which connects you to desperate spirits, and logically so when you think about it)* meditation, yoga, concentrated thought, or whatever system you might find and use, with prayer being the highest because you are seeking to move outside of yourself to connect to a more powerful energy system in God/Divine Architect/Creator, then your results are faster and more positive I find. Once you do that, the negative voices cannot reach you anymore because you operate on a higher frequency than they can reach, and you are then talking to a whole new group of folks. It is possible.

When you reach this point, you have control and access to all manner of information that only has usually come in snatches before, usually starting in childhood. If you were a child with premonitions that were inconsistent, then there is a possibility that you are not schizophrenic, but a medium in training. You just have to learn how to get control. That is not all people in this category, of course, but may be some.

If you can say the following prayer consistently - like 3 times a day for at least a month, really trying to understand what it means, even if you don't in the beginning, and the voices go away, seem confused *(remember that these are not just arbitrary voices, but actual spirit beings that you are communicating with -- this is the hard part because it takes rearranging the way you may have thought the world was organized*), or are less hostile or you hear them less often, then you are possibly, or perhaps a hazer. This is important. Never stop the prayer. It is like a control device to keep your vibrations high. As a medium, you will need such devices because of your vibratory differences.

Bear in mind, that in the beginning, possibly for the first two to three weeks, perhaps longer, they may get more hostile because they know you have gotten a system that might work, and that they won't be able to make your life miserable much longer, but they can't sustain the vibratory changes for long, so they will leave, or more accurately, you will leave them, vibratorily speaking. Couple this with burning a candle for your Guardian Angel/Spirit/Guide *(does not matter what your faith is - somebody is keeping track of you - - trust me on this for the moment)* and you may see major changes. If you do, it is likely that schizophrenia might not be what is happening but mediumship is. But this is tricky.

Please, DON'T go off of medication if you are on it. The changes will override the medication and you will need less of it as time goes on. Stay under the supervision of your medical practitioner, but do these things and the discomfort will generally change over time. You have nothing to lose from this perspective, if you do nothing foolish because of it, so just keep an open mind. Expect, that if you are diligent, you will feel quite different in about 6 to 8 months, a small price to pay if you've had years of this going on. I strongly suggest that you keep a journal, paying close attention to the hours after you say this particular prayer, and keeping track of the activity and content of the voices/spirits. Some will be stubborn.

I also suggest that you find a Sukyo Mahi Kari dojo (http://www.sukyomahikari.org/) and go to receive light regularly. They have them all over the world and they are free, with only service requested (like washing the windows or dusting), and/or a small donation if you have it. If not, no problem. I've worked with several clients now to separate these things and make the situation clearer. It doesn't matter if you believe it or not at first. What do you have to lose if the voices are making your life miserable? If you simply get out of your own ego and try it, you are likely to see changes. It is this element though, I will say, that is the hardest for people to work past if they are resistant. Your choice, but you do have a choice. If you can find a good, well trained Pranic Healer, this should be useful as well. They too are all over the world. http://www.pranichealing.com/ If you are a hazer, you are dealing with an alternate energy state, so it makes sense that a person, or system of alternate energy control might be beneficial for you.

Remember, and this is KEY! Self-involvement, self-pity, anger and frustration will keep you in this perpetual state because they are automatic vibration lowering devices. You will remain a hamster in a wheel unless you work to break this cycle, and that is what the vibration raisers mentioned before will do. It is not as hard as it might seem, in fact it is simple, but requires consistency and getting out of your ego. That is what the Hindu prayer will help you do. Say it even if you don't understand it, and one day, it will almost magically kick in and you will get what it is really about!

Here is the prayer below. Write me at evaravenwood@yahoo.com for the Guardian Angel altar information, as it needs more explanation. If you want to understand this better, I strongly suggest that you get my book **The Next God** or learn more about me at www.evaravenwood.com_ as the book explains not only my journey, but my mother's to some degree. I am also putting together a questionnaire for interested people, so that I can better distinguish some of the behavior and activities that people who hear voices undergo, so that I can identify hazers more efficiently. So please consider becoming part of this study, and contact me. I will send you the questionnaire once I finish compiling it, and appreciate in advance, your participation.

Think of it like getting through the hazing phase of a fraternity. If you get through it, there is a lot of wonderful stuff on the other side!

Be well and thank you for allowing me to be of possible service in this.
Eva

The Living Dead

Have done with pride and arrogance, conceit, envy, self- assertion;
Practice humility, obedience; worship the Creator.
When a man has abandoned false pride, arrogance and vainglory,
When he has become humble and meek, then does he find true bliss.
Prince and beggar alike must die: not one survives.
Him do thou call living who has died and yet lives.
My enemy "I" is dead: now none can smite me down.
'Tis I who slay myself: thus, being dead, I live.
We have slain our enemy, we have died; but he is not forgotten.
The thorn remains to vex us. Consider and lay this truth to heart.
Then only wilt thou find the Beloved when thou art as the living dead;
Only by losing thyself canst thou find Him who knoweth all.
Then wilt thou find the Beloved when thou esteemeth thyself as nothing;
Recognize therefore by quiet reflection whence the thought of self arises.
Becoming as the living dead, come thou into the way,
First lay down thy head, then mayest thou venture to plant thy foot.
Know that the way of discipleship is exceeding hard;
The living dead walk in it, the Name of Rama their sign.
So difficult is the way, no living man can tread it;
He only can walk in it, O foolish one, who has died and lives.
Only he who is dead can tread the way that leads to Niranjana;
He finds the Beloved, and leaps the fearsome gulf.

He that is alive shall die: only by dying inwardly shall he meet the Lord;
Forsaking his fellowship who can endure when trouble comes?
O when will this dominion of self pass away? When will the heart forget every other?
When will it be wholly refined? When will it find its true home?
When I am not, then there is one; when I intrude, then two.
When the curtain of "I" and "you" is drawn aside, then do I become ever as I was.

This prayer is found in the book "Every Eye Beholds You - A World Treasury of Prayer" with interfaith prayers from all over the world, edited by Thomas J. Craughwell. It, or one like it, is essential if you are going to make this journey of elevation, even if you are schizophrenic or bi-polar fully, and not just in hazing.

What Readers Say About *THE NEXT GOD* . . .

Every once in awhile a book comes along that captures your attention in a special way. Eva Ravenwood's *The Next God* has been such a work for me. Eva has trail-blazed a truly remarkable spiritual path. She courageously shares many insights and tools from her unique life and experiences in this inspiring, thought-provoking work. Any spiritual seeker will find it illuminating and engaging.

Rev. Maria Dancing Heart
Author of The Last Adventure Of Life

Eva Ravenwood makes an astonishing debut with an honest, straight-forward, lucid and fascinating account of life as a Direct -- one of thousands who bear the tremendous burden and blessing of being able to communicate with God directly and with Spirits on The Other Side. Ravenwood charts her own spiritual development and foibles and makes it clear that while she may be able to communicate with God, she is just as prone to being resistant to Her/His/Its guidance, although not for long because she has found that the consequences are just too great. Ravenwood addresses concepts such as Good and Evil, Ego and organized religion. The reader is treated to a grounded discussion of past lives and present missions. This is an easy, informative, and accessible read. There is something in this book for most everyone. For the everyday person, for seasoned explorers of the paranormal and the metaphysical, for the agnostic, the atheist and/or The True Believer... whether that belief is rooted in Christianity, Judaism, Buddhism, Islam or any number of belief systems.

Tua Nefer – Social Activist

This book is amazing, like none I have ever read, yet it was quick and easy to understand. Eva Ravenwood shares truths that are typically hard-learned in a lifetime by way of her own experiences and dialogues with others. I loved the tone and the layout of each chapter. Her book confirms so much and provides a direction for one's own spiritual journey. I highly recommend buying this book.

Kai B. - Spiritual Seeker

Wow!!!!!!! I read your book. I can't express to you how marvelous I thought it was! It was an unexpected surprise, as I was "resistant" when you first suggested it as the answers to my questions. You did a wonderful job and you are a great writer. I couldn't put it down. I think so much of what you have written and am usually not very good at expressing my feelings. I hope that you take these comments as complete truth as there is no "fluff" and actually more to it that I can relay here. You were right!!! Thank you, thank you, thank you!! I do appreciate what you have brought to light for me.

Jessica A. - Spiritual Seeker

Amazing honesty and brilliance in one place. This book shows a clarity very few people can attain. Eva shares hard gained wisdom and shows the path to God and how the universe function. If you are even mildly curious get this book it will explain more than you ever thought possible, and if you are already on the path read this, read this, read this......it will answer so many of the questions stuck in your head. Thanks Eva.

Colin Clayton – Spiritual Seeker

As a grieving mother who had recently lost my son, I found Eva's THE NEXT GOD incredibly comforting. I had looked to other authors on similar spiritual texts, but I found Eva disarmingly honest and her sincerity on her own search rang true for me. I am convinced Eva has important insights for anyone willing to suspend traditional WASP theories and accept the unfamiliar.

M – Spiritual Seeker